The Postmodern
Fuentes

The Postmodern Fuentes

Chalene Helmuth

Lewisburg
Bucknell University Press
London: Associated University Presses

Associated University Presses
440 Forsgate Drive
Cranbury, NJ 08512

Associated University Presses
16 Barter Street
London WC1A 2AH, England

Associated University Presses
P.O. Box 338, Port Credit
Mississauga, Ontario
Canada L5G 4L8

The paper used in this publication meets the requirements of the American National Standard for Permanence of Paper for Printed Library Materials Z39.48–1984.

Library of Congress Cataloging-in-Publication Data

Helmuth, Chalene, 1965–
    The postmodern Fuentes / Chalene Helmuth.
      p. cm.
    Includes bibliographical references (p.   ) and index.
    ISBN 0-8387-5322-1 (alk. paper)
    1. Fuentes, Carlos—Criticism and interpretation.
2. Postmodernism (Literature)—Mexico. I. Title.
PQ7297.F793Z69 1997
863—dc20
                           96-20484
                           CIP

PRINTED IN THE UNITED STATES OF AMERICA

To Henry and Esther

Contents

Acknowledgments

I AM GRATEFUL FOR THE SUPPORT LENT ME BY SEVERAL INDIVIDUALS throughout the writing process: Daniel Reedy, who first oriented me toward this topic; Susan de Carvalho, for her unfailing support expressed in many tangible ways; Steve Weisenburger, who capably led the way into postmodernism; John Kronik, for productively inquisitive interactions; and Mary E. Davis, for her sage encouragement. Thanks to all of you.

Special thanks are due Adolfo Castañón, at the Fondo de Cultura Económica, who was kind enough to grant permission to cite from *Cristóbal Nonato*.

Introduction

CARLOS FUENTES HAS BEEN AT THE FOREFRONT OF INNOVATIVE Spanish-American fiction since the publication of his first novel, *La región más transparente* [Where the air is clear], in 1958. He rose to worldwide prominence with the novel *La muerte de Artemio Cruz* [The death of Artemio Cruz] (1962), and is a central figure of the Boom, alongside Gabriel García Márquez, Julio Cortázar, Mario Vargas Llosa, and José Donoso, among others.

The trajectory of this Spanish-American explosion in formal experimentation as well as in market factors is well documented.[1] The first novels of the Boom are written in the fifties; the critical consensus is that the movement's peak occured in the sixties. Their literary antecedents include James Joyce and William Faulkner; the novels appear on the heels of existential angst, complicated by events leading to the chaos of World War II. Addressing the distinctive features of the Boom, Donald Shaw points to the radical questioning of two central elements—reality and the writer's task: "This questioning is seen as having led to the rejection of old-style realism, with its simple assumptions about time and cause and effect, and to its replacement on the one hand by a heightened sense of the mystery and ambiguity of things, and on the other by greater reliance on fantasy and the creative imagination."[2] It is from this fertile field that Carlos Fuentes reaps his prolific body of work.

Fuentes, along with these writers from various regions of Spanish America, places his novels within recognizably Spanish-American realities; yet the implications of their thematic concerns of the novels are clearly universal. For the first time in history, autochthonous Spanish-American narratives, encased in refreshingly innovative forms, are read by a large, international public. The effects are momentous, as numerous translations proliferate and as the techniques are recognized for their unique contributions to world literature. *La muerte de Artemio Cruz*, for instance, is structured by dislocated chronology; the narrative perspective is refracted into three voices, and questions of identity are treated within the fragmentation of a disin-

11

tegrating self. The protagonist is a Mexican individual dealing with the aftermath of the Revolution and U.S. intervention, thus placing the novel in a recognizably Spanish-American context.

The phenomenon of the Boom irrevocably changed Spanish-American letters. However, to gain an accurate understanding of the current textual production of this region, one must also acknowledge the seminal contributions of the Cuban neobaroque (the works of José Lezama Lima, Severo Sarduy, and Guillermo Cabrera Infante), too little known outside Hispanist circles. The contribution of these writers is particularly evident on a linguistic level, as they exploit the instability of the sign. The result is, in the words of Roberto González Echevarría, a "mortal masquerade" brought about by "speculation about secondariness, about the primacy of the copy, about the persistence of the model in the copy . . . a Baroque spectacle."[3] These texts are exuberantly fragmented, a refraction and disfiguration of traditional narrative elements; the characters seem "to have been born *ad hoc* for fiction." (p. 64) The artificiality of the text is thereby explored and trumpeted alongside the more somber, existential matters being addressed in the novels of the continental Boom.

In 1975 Fuentes publishes *Terra Nostra*, a novel that Anglo critics regularly list as representative of Hispanic postmodern texts. It is a vast, encyclopedic novel that has been compared to Thomas Pynchon's *Gravity's Rainbow* in its scope and in its propensity towards multifarious versions of historical events and notions of the self. Following this, Fuentes has written (in addition to short stories) six novels and one collection of novellas to date, each of which can be best understood if examined in the context of contemporary postmodern textual expression.

The texts produced by Carlos Fuentes merit study in and of themselves, to the student of both Spanish-American and postmodern fiction. Yet they are particularly valuable in that this prolific body of work spans over forty years, reflecting contemporaneous changes in literary movements; and this novelistic trajectory models the evolution of form practiced in broad frontiers from modernism to postmodernism.

John Brushwood explains the temptation, especially among non-Spanish-American readers, to place the Boom in either modernist or postmodernist camps.[4] He argues against the imposition of such a paradigm on the grounds of complexity of the spectrum of Spanish-American texts. Brushwood acknowledges a transition in several Boom writers—among them, García Márquez and Donoso—from "representational fiction" to "an entirely different concept of the novel genre, one that accords reasonably well with the notion of Post-Modernism." (p. 23) Keith Booker has recently published a parallel study, examining the transition to postmodern expression in the fiction of Mario Vargas Llosa.

As the following analysis shows, Carlos Fuentes's novelistic production, particularly since 1975, gives ample evidence of postmodern features akin to those that appear in works of such Anglo American and European writers as Kathy Acker, Thomas Pynchon, John Barth, Robert Coover, Italo Calvino, Umberto Eco, Milan Kundera, and Salman Rushdie. Certainly, there is a growing contingent of Spanish-American writers—who join Boom writers still practicing their craft (principally Vargas Llosa and García Márquez)—whose postmodernism has clear and indisputable affinities with that of the writers listed above. Among the more recent writers whose works are recognizably within this mode of textual expression are Ricardo Piglia (Argentina), Gustavo Sáinz (Mexico), Diamela Eltit (Chile), and Abel Posse (Argentina), and Fernando del Paso (Mexico).

Postmodern Spanish-American texts should be viewed as counterparts to these other American and European texts, where mutual influence is exerted, and not as a localized imitation of the latest import from the North and from Europe. These texts do not appear as tardy results of foreign literary influences, but as contemporaneous, evolving forms originating from and redoubling upon a rich literary tradition that is firmly in place by midcentury.[5]

A study like the one that follows raises significant questions about the existence of Spanish-American postmodernism. Both Hispanist and Anglo critics have only very recently begun to explore these questions. For instance, is Spanish-American postmodernism distinct from U.S. or European postmodernism? I would affirm that it is, insofar as Calvino's is Italian, or Kundera's Czechoslovakian. Nonetheless, the irrefutable presence of certain consistent features points the way to clear affinities with what may be termed "worldwide" postmodern literature. There is certainly much room for increased critical discussion of these matters, to which this study is intended to contribute.

The division of the study into chapters that separately address each novel allows for their comprehensive examination, as well as for a comparative assessment of these post-1975 works. The first chapter considers Fuentes's early works (1958–68), and provides an introduction to the postmodern theory of texts that will structure the approach of the following chapters. Chapter One ends with a discussion of *Terra Nostra* (1975), a watershed in Fuentes's novelistic trajectory that initiates perspectives evident in each of his subsequent novels to date.

Chapter Two analyzes the means by which *Una familia lejana* [Distant relations] (1980) makes the narrative act its subject; the self-reflexivity of the novel provides an intertextual guide to Fuentes' other works. In following chapters, *La cabeza de la hidra* [The hydra head] (1978) utilizes the conventions of the spy genre to problematize the process of individuation, with serious implications for configurations of the modern self. Similarly, the fetus-narrator of *Cristóbal Nonato* [Christopher Unborn] (1987) combines an unlikely narrative premise with the reader's positioning as an active participant in determining the events of narration. The transfer of narrative control to the reader serves Fuentes's intent to present alternate versions of the text.

As a historical account, *Gringo viejo* [The old Gringo] (1985) includes the subjective, atemporal plane of dreams and memory in its version of the events of the past. The novel subverts the traditional conventions of historical recounting in its equal treatment of the internal and external realms. *La campaña* [The campaign] (1990) installs and subverts the conventions of myth in its recounting of the past. Fuentes's narrator admits to his subjective rendering of events; this historical work exposes the motivated nature of historical accounts. Chapter Five concludes with a discussion of these recent works by Fuentes: subscribing to the postmodern dissolution of authoritative constructs, they leave their inner contradictions unresolved, projecting a plurality of truths.

I conclude with a brief summary of the telling features of a collection of novellas, *El naranjo, o los círculos del tiempo* [The orange tree] (1993), as well as Fuentes's 1994 novel, *Diana, o la cazadora solitaria* [The goddess who hunts alone]. These texts definitively continue the postmodern vein detailed in the following analysis.

To readers familiar with the novels of the Boom and its considerable scholarship, this study provides a guide to understanding Fuentes's interest in questions of an epistemological and ontological nature that he continues to explore through technically experimental fiction. A discussion of Fuentes within the context of postmodern literary expression clarifies his intent, and provides a solid base for new readings of his fiction, both before and after 1975.

Carlos Fuentes is a recognized innovator of texts; the present study establishes an important base of comparison and association with current trends. in textual experimentation. We then reaffirm the permanent contribution of Carlos Fuentes to Spanish-American fiction in particular, and to world literature in general.

The Postmodern
Fuentes

1

Approaching Postmodernism: From *La región más transparente* (1958) to *Terra Nostra* (1975)

As THE BEST-KNOWN CONTEMPORARY MEXICAN NOVELIST, CARLOS Fuentes has contributed significantly to the innovations of Spanish-American literature. His literary production covers a wide range of genres including the short story, drama, essay, and novel. Although his first publication was a collection of short stories, *Los días enmascarados* [The masked days] (1954), Fuentes attracted popular and critical attention with his first novel, *La región más transparente* (1958). The novel was of interest due to its unique portrayal of urban Mexico. Set in the 1950s, it makes real the Aztec presence of hundreds of years earlier through several characters who embody those ancient values, beliefs, and traditions, and by means of the Indian symbols of rite and sacrifice that appear throughout the novel. This thematic interest in Mexico, identity, and the interplay of past and present reappears consistently in subsequent works.

His third novel, *La muerte de Artemio Cruz* (1962), is one whose thematic and stylistic concerns place him at the forefront of the Spanish-American Boom of the sixties. This period explores existential questions in works that reflect in their form the consequent confusion and disruption of previously held perceptions. Technical experimentation includes the undermining of the traditional concept of time through such devices as circularity, juxtaposition of events, and otherwise dislocated chronology; multiple and shifting narrative stances; and an emphasis on language not as a reflection of reality but as a force capable of creating its own reality.

Critics frequently cite *Artemio Cruz* as illustrating characteristic Boom expressions. The protagonist lies on his deathbed and reviews the events of his life, as the different voices within him reflect on what he has become—a self-interested businessman who has rejected the ideals of the Mexican Revolution, ideals for which he had fought fifty years earlier. The events of his life are recounted in twelve episodes but in disrupted order, so that causality is undermined; his voice is divided into three, each representing a different part of his psyche, thus depicting the fragmented condition of modern man. The novel was immediately recognized for its significance in the Spanish-American novel's breakthrough into world literature, like the Russian novel in the late nineteenth century with Dostoevsky and Tolstoy, and the English-language novel of the twenties and thirties with Joyce and Faulkner. Fuentes's novelistic production continues through the sixties with *Aura* (1962), *Zona sagrada* [Holy place] (1968), *Cambio de piel* [A change of skin] (1967), and *Cumpleaños* [Birthday] (1969), novels that are consistently experimental in their thematic and formal explorations of time, identity, and fiction. It is *Terra Nostra* (1975), however, that once again captures the attention of readers worldwide, and serves to place Fuentes at the forefront of Spanish-American postmodern expression.

The novel is a fictionalized account of Spanish history that begins in 1999 and goes back to the sixteenth century in the age of King Philip II. A mock historical novel, it moves from the discovery of the New World to the days of the rule of Tiberius, introducing many recognizable figures, both historical and literary. It represents an enormous narrative feat in its incorporation of a rich diversity of themes, and draws on an immense body of world literature through intertextual references. Essential to the novel's theme as well as to its form is its use of perspective. Philip's is a univocal perspective that follows the medieval hierarchical cosmovision, with God above and Man below. Absolute authority rests with God and, by extension, with Philip II as divinely appointed King. The discovery of another world threatens his views because it involves the admission of perspectives different from his own. Plurality intrudes on a king who is unprepared to handle the possibilities of previously unconceived realities.

The novel's further representations of the self, time, reading, fiction, and other constructs make it evident that its author is pushing this genre to previously untested limits. His seven subsequent texts to date, *La cabeza de la hidra* (1978), *Una familia lejana* (1980), *Gringo viejo* (1985), *Cristóbal Nonato* (1987), *La campaña* (1990), *El naranjo, o los círculos del tiempo* (1993), and *Diana, o la cazadora solitaria* (1994), continue in this direction of pushing toward new extremes in novelistic intent and form. Although they are consistent with earlier novels' postulations about identity, time, and fiction, the novels written after 1975 reflect a discernible change in his literary representation of these constructs.

In a lecture delivered at a North American university, Carlos Fuentes presented a sketch of the perspectives that have guided his recent novelistic production.[1] His comments are particularly relevant to his latest fiction, beginning with Terra Nostra. Entitled "The Power of the Written Word," the lecture underscored the vital role of literature in its dual function of naming and of giving voice as it reveals "a constellation of constant questions related to the creation of our culture." The author spoke of the importance of literature in keeping the past alive and at the forefront of readers' minds, thus acknowledging his characteristic preoccupation with the debt of the present and the future to the past; he stated, "There is no living future with a dead past." These elements—of questioning and of the past—have long been acknowledged by readers of Fuentes as inherent to his thematic concerns, and they continue to appear in his latest fiction. The emphasis of the lecture, however, points to new perspectives evident in works from Terra Nostra to the present, pespectives that situate Fuentes within a worldwide movement in literature.

The novels of Carlos Fuentes from 1975 to the present have in common an urgency about the crises of modernity, where individuals find themselves confronted with such an enormous span of constructs that they begin to question what is real and what is not. They are faced with the almost inconceivable plurality of a world that is increasingly diverse. As Fuentes states:

> Literature is an expression of the cultural, personal, and spiritual diversity of humankind. It cannnot express this diversity if it only expresses one truth. The written word is a harbinger of a multipolar and multicultural world where no single philosophy, no single belief, no single solution can shove aside or replace the extreme wealth of the cultural heritage that all of us . . . have been able to create since the beginning of time.[2]

For Carlos Fuentes, those who write must train the reader to develop a vision that admits that multiplicity of truths, shunning by implication the univocal and the absolute. Fuentes's comments recall the chief claims made for postmodern art.

The implications for his fiction are tremendous, for the absence of these traditional voices of authority allows great freedom in presenting alternate versions of language and literature and, by extension, of reality. Carlos Fuentes intends through his fiction to present a multiplicity of possibilities; language, character, and in fact the entire narrative are textual representations of humankind's need to define itself in the face of the loss of the absolute. Literature oscillates between reflecting and creating reality; fiction gains in ontological status because it, too, forms its own reality: it is not simply a falsely transparent mirroring of what lies outside the literary text. The existence of a "multipolar and multicultural" world requires that individual identity leave itself open to the possibility of otherness, to possess definition only temporarily, and to incorporate other elements into itself as each individual is only a transient self. Thus postmodern writers often focus on the narrative representation of character, as a reflection of the extratextual status of the self.

Although postmodernism resists a final definition, it does provide an orientation within which to examine these writers' questioning of perceptions and depictions of reality. Fundamental to their concerns is a preoccupation with modernity on all accounts. For the purposes of this study, the following considerations of postmodernism will be used.

Postmodernism may be conceived as an appraisal of the contemporary from a constructed distance. The inherent paradox of this claim of objectivity stems from the fact that the outsider is necessarily situated within modernity. The modern provides focus for the postmodern; the assumptions of modernity are brought to the surface and examined, at times in the light of the past. At other times, these elements of modernity are held in dialectical patterns (of the self versus others, of high versus popular art, for instance), often through the displacement of the central or the centering of the marginal. At the heart of postmodernism is a process of continual challenge to anything that lays claim to the absolute. Postmodernism itself offers scarce conclusions about the contemporary, since to do so would invalidate its commitment to challenging, if not refuting, any one voice that imposes itself on others.

Linda Hutcheon explains the paradoxes of postmodernism as "modernist aesthetic autonomy and self-reflexivity that come up against a counterforce in the form of a grounding in the historical, social, and political world."[3] She accurately assesses in her discussion the preoccupation of postmodernity both with literary craft and with the world. The traditional modernist separation of high art forms and mass culture is demolished in confronting external realities within the text. As to the contradictions of postmodernism, Hutcheon values them as differentiating characteristics that emphasize postmodernism's own advocacy of plurality. Its orientation is much broader; it encompasses artist as well as art form.

Critics have found it both useful and necessary to describe the postmodern orientation in terms of its relationship to modernism. Although some theorists have proposed an oppositional scheme to represent the relationship between the two,[4] it is evident that postmodernism is not a simple reaction to modernism; it borrows from it, challenges it, and incorporates its techniques, although there is always an attempt to push them to new limits. The postmodernist appropriation of technique involves an ongoing interplay in which authors move in and out of the modernist technical mode, but for very different reasons than those of the modernists. John Barth states: "As for twentieth century literary postmodernism, I date it from when many of us stopped worrying about the death of the novel (a Modernist worry) and began worrying about the death of the reader—and of the planet—instead."[5] By pushing modernist devices to their limits, the implications of the postmodern are more disturbing than the death of the novel. The extremism of postmodernist use of technical devices reflects the acute perception that temporality, authority, and selfhood are at stake.

In Brian McHale's terms, postmodernism involves a change of dominant from epistemological to ontological questioning.[6] The questions no longer address our speculations about understanding the systems of reality; the present dilemma is whether these systems exist at all. While modernists would transfer epistemological difficulties to the reader through dislocated chronology and the withholding of information (p. 9), for instance, postmodernists might incorporate this as a given of the modern world. Not only would no solution be offered, the postmodernist would further challenge the notion of a coherent reality. Modernist devices of interior monologue, experimentation with language, or nonlinearity might thus be used to present the reader with the relativity not just of an individual perception but of all perceptions. The design of the author, then, is to reveal that there is in fact no standard reality to which we can conclusively attribute coherence and meaning. In Fuentes's own words, "the only truth is the search for truth;"[7] at a loss for conclusions, the postmodern prefers to examine the formation of suppositions rather than attempt to lead us to conclusions.

Postmodernism also furthers modernist self-awareness as fiction to a *modus operandi* based on the perception that fiction is yet another discourse by which we construct reality; it is informed by critical theories of the late twentieth century that have irrevocably changed writers'—and readers'—view of textual production. In its departure from the modernist conception of art as above the commonplace, reserved incestuously for those who produce it, the text can be examined in terms of its process of formation. In postmodern writing, fiction is offered as an instance of reality-as-process. The narrative act itself and the textual space become a commentary on our extra-textual construction of reality. Extreme self-reflexivity and self-consciousness, then, are hallmarks of postmodernist writing.

At the level of characterization, some postmodern writers project characters into a new level of the text so that they themselves either create other characters, modify existing ones, or create new fictions that somehow alter the course of narration. Jorge Luis Borges's short story, "Las ruinas circulares," [The circular ruins] illustrates this technique, as one character develops from the mental projection of another. A character becomes a lens through which light passes, refracting itself into others, diffusing the writer's own creation, as the created is endowed with the power to create. This technique of focalization is an important element in fictionalization.

Modernism, then, plays a fundamental role in defining postmodernism, and the difference between these two movements can be said to be largely a difference of degree. Always conscious of what precedes it, postmodernism holds modernism and its devices in a critical light. Its incorporation of modernist technique is often parodic, enabling the exteriorization of the assumptions from which the techniques have come. Never pacified by conclusions, postmodernism's appraisal of modernity constantly shifts to the constructs behind conclusions. Its texts identify and embody the processes that form our assumptions about time, the self, the nature of reality, and narrative representation.

The postmodern conception of history is also one of critical confrontation, not taking anything for granted as factual. Since historiography is a scripted fiction, history is also seen as a fictional construct. Therefore, the same considerations that apply to the narrative apply to history, and the past may be approached with the same ontological questions with which postmodernism confronts fiction.

Fuentes's works that deal with the past exemplify the dual

interest of postmodernist writing in fiction and history in its critical confrontation with the past. As Linda Hutcheon's term, "historiographic metafiction," suggests, these works are "intensely self-reflexive and yet paradoxically lay claim to historical events and personages" (p. 5). In *Gringo viejo*, for example, Fuentes constructs a possible ending to the life of a U.S.-Civil-War veteran and journalist, Ambrose Bierce, placing him within the turmoil of the Mexican Revolution, an actual historical event. The emphasis in the work, however, is on the fictionality of the world in which the characters exist. This world is the result of memory, which functions similarly to language in its construction of reality. In *Terra Nostra*, the events of the New World's discovery are related from a distance that Mendelson calls both prophetic and satiric,[8] but they are woven within a text that knows itself to be a fictional construct. Like *Gringo viejo*, this work provides liberal commentary on the process it is describing, treating history much like fiction. The process of memory—recalling, evoking, recreating—provides an awareness of its status as narrative construct.

At the level of narrative, the self-reflexive distance that is characteristic of postmodernism often takes the form of parody. This affects not only the selection of technique, but also the narrative act and the concept of genre—in short, any aspect of fiction. In *La cabeza de la hidra*, Fuentes constructs a narration within the framework of a detective story. The genre is subverted by basing the spies' code on Shakespearean epithets, thus inserting literary elitism into a popular form. In *Cristóbal Nonato*, on the other hand, the narrator's role is parodied through the increased responsibility of the reader. Addressed so frequently that he is given a name that combines his functions, the engendered reader, "Elector," is asked at one point to fill in a page that has been left blank, so that he may finish the episode to his liking.

Clearly, the questioning of previous orientations toward fiction, the critical confrontation of history, and the parody of all aspects of the narrative point to one of the central concepts of postmodernism: the notion of plurality. This perception involves the loss of absolutes so that indeterminacy is expected, and so that the only constants are change and the refutation of what was upheld as permanent. This is fundamental to the consideration of Carlos Fuentes as a postmodern writer, for he is always questioning reality and our perceptions of it. Among his novels written before 1975, *Cambio de piel* is the first to structure itself by means of this technique to the extremes that are characteristic of postmodernism. His textual representation of character in the novel, for instance, moves beyond fragmentation to the denial and the loss of self. Characters subsequent to *Cambio de piel* tend to be either products of focalization, metamorphosing figures,[9] or characters who share some transcendental mode of being (memory and conscience, for example). In essence, characters in the post-1975 works continue to represent figures that have lost the autonomy and form of individual identity.

The act of narration shares the loss of autonomy, as it is desecrated and is no longer the domain of the narrator. It can be appropriated by either the reader or the characters themselves. *Una familia lejana* makes narration not merely a vehicle but the subject of its fiction when the narrator's univocal status breaks down; he discusses the narration with the reader, thereby exposing the process of textual creation. Again, plurality facilitates the exploration of the process, which is now much more important than are the conclusions.

Plurality is expressed textually in other ways as well. In *Cristóbal Nonato*, the shifts between characters are deliberately ambiguous so as to confuse the readers' perspective. Forcing them to delay judgement or misleading the readers, the narrator leads them to an awareness of how susceptible they are to the appropriation of unfounded assumptions. This is in line with the postmodern premise that precludes the imposition of any one view over another.

The narrative loss of autonomy occurs again as the textual voice is refracted to include different texts. Thus, intertextuality plays a significant role in the plurality of postmodernist fiction. Most of Fuentes's works from 1975 to 1990 include the layering of references within the text, resulting in variegated patters of textual expression.

(Somewhat) finally, the subversion of endings advocates plurality in the postmodern fiction of Carlos Fuentes. In *Una familia lejana*, the story is carried on as the future transmission of the narration becomes the reader's responsibility. Harriet Winslow of *Gringo viejo* sits and remembers; her activity is a part of the timeless realm of memory, suggesting endless motion. The first scene of *La cabeza de la hidra* is identical to the last. Postmodernism's deferral of conclusions is formally underscored with endings that do not end.

Thus, it is clear that the novels subsequent to *Terra Nostra* represent the writer's increasing identification with matters of interest to the postmodernists. Although his literary production to that point explores questions of an epistemological as well as of an ontological nature, *Terra Nostra* represents a watershed in Fuentes's writing, involving the expansion of these questions to exceed previous limits. The fragmentation of self becomes the loss of self. The refraction of the narrative voice goes beyond reflecting the cacophony of modernity: it points to plurality as the necessary norm. Where in prior literary movements the present is examined in the light of the past, the past itself is now reexamined as a fictional construct. Where conclusions were previously unintelligible, they now are either openly subverted, or are not offered at all, as postmodernism displaces its focus to the postulations behind conclusions.

Terra Nostra represents Carlos Fuentes's first great experiment with postmodern notions of plurality, after which he diversifies his exploration of postmodernist themes. He moves toward extracting the process from existing conclusions, rethinking the past in terms of the present, and considering the contemporary from a perspective that is always aware of its own stance, shifting continuously to allow for full expression of plurality. Thus, the postmodern perspectives evident in Fuentes's later novels come into their own with the appearance of *Terra Nostra*, yet this trajectory from modern to postmodern is marked by gradual change, with the inclusion in one text of an increasingly radical or nontraditional element that is more fully developed in a later text. To illustrate, a brief overview of Carlos Fuentes's novelistic production follows.

The past figures significantly in all of Fuentes's works. *La región más transparente* (1958) and *La muerte de Artemio Cruz* (1962) situate their narratives within postrevolutionary Mexico and relate present conditions, both personal and social, to events and perspectives formed during the Revolution nearly fifty years earlier. Thus, the past continues as a living force, still exerting its influence on the present.

In the later novels, the past takes on a different character, one that is much more malleable and less accountable to the consensus of historians. *Terra Nostra* (1975) sets its story during the time of the discovery of the New World but moves to different historical periods, juxtaposing time frames and transposing characters from one era to another. *Gringo viejo* (1985) is written as a memory of the Mexican Revolution, and *La campaña* (1990) recalls the early nineteenth-century Spanish-American independence movements. But both novels create new versions of history in the process of remembering.

While the portrayal of history changes gradually from the first novels to the latest to date, *Terra Nostra* (1975) represents a fork in the road—one with multiple prongs—with which Fuentes initiates a decidedly postmodern textual mode of expression. The earlier works challenge any vision of the present that does not include a consideration of the past. History is seen as fundamental to an understanding of oneself and to the formation of identity, and Fuentes explores this concept at both individual and collective levels. This perspective is accentuated in later novels by Fuentes's presentation of history not as factual record, but as the product of memory. Thus, no longer is the consideration of history possible without recognizing its status as a subjective, narrative procedure occurring within the present. History is at the same time influenced by and exerting its influence on the present.

Fuentes undermines the traditional concept of time to illustrate history's change of status from static and absolute to variable. Although chronological disruption is common to most of his novels, beginning with *La muerte de Artemio Cruz*, the subsequent novels move towards a more radical rupturing of time. The characters in *Aura* (1962) are on opposite ends of a linear conception of time (the young Aura embodies the former self of Consuelo, who is eighty years old), yet they converge at a point of simultaneity. The narrative of *Cumpleaños* (1969) aligns lives through reincarnation, thereby breaking barriers of time and space. Characters experience a descent into uncertainty as they lose the bearings previously provided by the regular succession of time.

In *Terra Nostra*, the parameters of time are pushed to new extremes in an attempt to challenge any definitive view of the temporal. This novel gives an inaccurate account of a well-known historical event to illustrate the possibility of alternate reconstructions of history. The factor of time itself—as the standard by which events are judged to be either in the present or in the past—eventually becomes one more subjective construct.

Novels subsequent to *Terra Nostra* experiment with the indeterminacy of temporality. *Una familia lejana* (1980), particularly, evokes a world outside of the notions of time, where characters slip into a temporal framework momentarily, thus exposing the status of time as an imposed construct. The fetus-narrator of *Cristóbal Nonato* (1987) speaks from within the atemporal womb, and he must undergo an instant's forgetting of all he knows before he may begin to live outside the womb and within a temporal framework.

In challenging the common perceptions of reality, not only does Fuentes subjectify historical fact and chronological time in ways that progressively destroy their authority, but the notion of the self is undermined as well. As he has done with the concept of time since the earliest works, Fuentes challenges traditional means of characterization. His first novel, *La región más transparente*, offers a collective portrait of society through a collage of characters; the novel's protagonist is, in effect, Mexican society fifty years after the Revolution. *La muerte de Artemio Cruz* turns its focus to an individual's introspection at the end of his life. The narrative splits the protagonist's voice into three, so that in this second novel the external diffusion is turned inward. A society that is offered as a collective protagonist is thus only symptomatic of the fragmented condition of the individual represented by Artemio Cruz. In *Cambio de piel*, the refraction of the self becomes central as four characters' stories are woven through each other, confusing the distinctions between them and distorting the concept of character. This anticipates the loss of the self, which is particularly the focus of works by Carlos Fuentes after 1975. Thus, we can observe a trajectory within Fuentes's literary production wherein the fragmented notions of one novel become a central theme or medium of the next; consequently these elements are refracted once again, creating perspectives and models that are continually new.

EARLY WORKS 1958–1962

Each of the first four novels by Fuentes clearly reflects the different stages in his literary trajectory. What is consistent, however, is the intent to experiment continually with new styles and means of presentation.[10] Formally as well as thematically, the novels of this period move from the modernist prose of *La región más transparente* (1958); to the Galdosian style of mimetic, realist representation of *Las buenas conciencias* [The good conscience] (1959); to the technical experimentation of the Boom in *La muerte de Artemio Cruz* (1962), one of this movement's most representative works; and to Gothic presentation in *Aura* (1962). Characteristic of the first four novels are the thematic concerns that remain at the forefront of the author's production to date: time and identity. Although they are encased in differing formal presentations that demonstrate an evolution in style, these thematic concerns remain the same throughout Fuentes's works.

Fuentes's first novel provides a wide-angle view of Mexican society, providing a sweeping glance over its different components. As readers, we hear fragments of conversations that take place in disjointed chronological order, and shift among situations that occur simultaneously at different junctures of society. This stylistic rendering of a postrevolutionary society suffering from radical upheaval portrays the attempt at forging a new Mexican identity from the standpoint of different members of the society.

Federico Robles's high-power economic dealings with foreign investors are plagued by falsehood and betrayal, and he is condemned as much for ignoring his Indian origins as he is for neglecting to carry out the ideals of the Revolution. Members of the lower strata of society cross the Río Grande in search of relief from poverty but always return to Mexico, their prosperity only momentary. Ixca Cienfuegos, the embodiment of the past in its indigenous, timeless beliefs, is cunning in his role as reminder of the truth and of the essence that each character is in some manner tempted to disregard. The conclusion of the novel portrays great sacrifice, even death, as necessary punishment for those who forget their past as well as for those who ignore their essential being. Fuentes, then, discusses the problematics of identity in relation to the burden of history.

The style of *Región* may be compared to John Dos Passos's high-modernist prose of the *USA Trilogy*, as it depicts the different strata of a society in a collage. Its impressionistic technique and fragmentary presentation combine form with message in the modernist tradition. Like Dos Passos's novels, *Región* demonstrates the perspectives of a society that is newly diverse, experiencing the changes effected by war and immigration, so that the questioning of the factors that define an American or a Mexican becomes central.

Carlos Fuentes's novel also depicts this loss of unity and the threat of increased differentiation; yet he adds an element omnipresent in his novels and absent in Dos Passos's: the factor of the past, which for Fuentes weighs heavily on every subsequent time. The effect is one of intensified fragmentation, as the past becomes another force to be reckoned with in an ever-diverse world.

Fuentes's second novel, *Las buenas conciencias* (1959), has largely failed to capture the interest of critics. It offers little formal innovation, which is an element Fuentes's readers have perhaps come to expect. The novel is written in the form of a bildungsroman and develops in chronological order, using traditional means of characterization. It has been labeled a reflection of Fuentes's own coming of age, and is generally dismissed as a necessary but insignificant product of his development as a writer. This novel does, however, provide a contrast to his recent works as significant as the difference between traditional realist nineteenth and late twentieth-century novels.

La muerte de Artemio Cruz (1962) must be considered within the context of the Spanish-American Boom. As part of this movement, one may consider the importance of the form of the novel, as part of its message. Artemio Cruz responds well to this categorization in its treatment of the fragmentation of the modern self. The narrative voice is divided into three—first, second, and third person—each speaking for a different component of Artemio Cruz's person.

The "I" narrates the thoughts and feelings of the protagonist as he lies on his deathbed and experiences physical pain. It serves as the expression of a seventy-year-old man who now hears two other voices that evoke scenes from the past and that serve as a reminder of views and beliefs that were once a part of him. The years after the war have changed him, so that the revolutionary ideals he fought for have been abandoned. The third-person narration provides an objective account of events as they occurred in the past, yet in disjointed chronological order, so that the fragmented, piecemeal quality of his life is formally underscored.

Finally, the second person narrative voice directly addresses the protagonist and, as Lanin Gyurko and others have pointed out, represents the voice of his conscience.[11] It is condemnatory in tone, for Artemio Cruz has consistently shut it out and acted unscrupulously throughout his life after the war. As part of himself, though, the "tú" represents a plea for Artemio's divided self to become one again; but as he dies, we come to realize that this return to wholeness is impossible until the epiphanic moment of death, when the three parts coalesce.

Developing partially from the modernist tradition that brings the subconscious to the surface through the technical device of stream of consciousness, Fuentes and other Boom writers turn to the subconscious in order to gain a more accurate comprehension of the self. The flowing pattern, rather than ordered syntax, is important in tracing the evolution of Fuentes's writing. In Región, the conversations were depicted as fragmentary; in *Artemio Cruz* they progress to an even freer representation spanning three perspectives, each represented by a different narrative voice. This technique later evolves into seemingly senseless word meanderings in *Cambio de piel* and in *Cristóbal Nonato* (1987).

The linguistic freedom from consciously ordered patterns is an important one: the subversion of language, as a logical construct, allows nonrational expression. The subconscious, the mythical, the archetypal, and the fragmentary are thus afforded verbal representation. Consistent with Fuentes's interest in the creative force of language, these early works represent a crucial transitional period of experimentation with linguistic form.

Artemio Cruz is defined by his response to external situations: his imprisonment during the Revolution; Regina's death; the opportunity to blackmail Gamaliel; his marriage to Catalina; his son Lorenzo's death. Although causality is undermined by the dislocated chronology, the external grid of the Revolution and the ensuing upheaval in Mexican society, imposed upon Artemio Cruz, is an important force in his fragmentation.

This consequence is significant as a forerunner of Fuentes' postulation evident in his later novels (post-*Cambio de piel*), that the unity of the self is no longer feasible. A postmodern view, this crisis of selfhood becomes a focal point of Fuentes's novelistic production. The early works undertake an exploration of fragmented identity with external causes. The two novels that follow oscillate between external and internal factors. The human condition is due to a collective and unavoidable refraction of personhood through the incorporation of increasing levels of reality and of temporal and spatial planes. Therefore, multiplicity becomes the mode of being, no longer viewed as an aberration, but part of a growing consciousness of its representation of the condition of the contemporary self.

TRANSITIONAL WORKS: ZONA SAGRADA (1967) AND CAMBIO DE
PIEL (1967)

Although they were published in the same year, *Zona sagrada* and *Cambio de piel* represent different stages in Fuentes's fiction. They depart from a similar formal base, one of radical experimentation with modernist technique, to achieve the effect of indeterminacy in their representation of individuals, a goal common to most postmodern works. Yet both novels function

within rational frameworks that serve to explain the radical nature of each text: the irregularities of Mito's characterization in
the first novel can be attributed to the context of mythical archetypes and a severe Oedipal fixation; and Freddy Lambert, the
narrator and one-time voice of authority in the second text,
writes from a lunatic asylum. Because of these rational explanations of the characters' irrationality, these two novels must be
considered as transitional, moving towards postmodern themes
and techniques but not yet breaking through traditional assumptions about reality and the self.

As Brian McHale notes, the dominant concerns in *Zona sagrada* are epistemological, focusing on the theme of illusion
versus reality (p. 16). As readers, we share the protagonist Guillermo's confusion in his confrontation with his world. There is
a confluence of realities as cinema, myth, and psychology converge, blending indistinguishably with external realities to expand the concept of reality itself. The incorporation of mythic
space admits a plurality of time and space and is corroborated
on a stylistic level by the alternating presence of autobiographical and dramatic styles and by a "mixture of tones—confessional, colloquial, lyrical, supplicatory, denunciatory."[12]

The principal characters in *Zona sagrada* are based on the
legendary Mexican movie star of the 1940s and 1950s, María
Félix (renamed Claudia Nervo in the novel), and her son Enrique
(Guillermo or, significantly, Mito). Mito spends much of the novel
pursuing Claudia or engaging in elaborate fantasies of her as his
lover, responding to him and sharing an intimate companionship. These fantasies serve as a respite from Mito's reality in
which Claudia has little interest in her son, and seems instead
to purposefully tease him, and to enjoy exercising her control
over him.

The story is narrated primarily as Mito's monologue. His Oedipal complex is the cause of severe distortions of perception; consequently the narration is often erratic, leaving events ambiguous
or unexplained. In addition, as Wendy F. Faris states, "nonrational modes of perception and communication—myths, rituals,
strange coincidences, dreams, obsessions, fantasies— . . . often
structure the narrative."[13] Thus, traditional modes of representation, clear and rational, are replaced with others that allow for a
different conceptualization of space (which becomes a sacred,
mythic region within which an individual can establish her own
territory), time, and character. Fuentes utilizes cinema, myth,

and psychological abnormality as creative vehicles for innovative characterization in *Zona sagrada*.

The cinematographic element figures significantly in Fuentes's depiction of Mito's movement within his world of indeterminate reality. He does not so much struggle to differentiate between illusion and reality, as he attempts to create a convincing illusion that for him is far more desirable than reality. Many scenes revolve around her filmmaking episodes, and Mito typically fantasizes playing the lead role opposite his mother, Claudia. He is obsessed with her screen roles, and plays them over and over again in his apartment, feeding his fantasies and further insulating his world from the outside. Movie-viewing provides Mito access to a world of illusion that he appropriates without question as reality.

Mito's creation of a reality often takes the form of a scene in which he is the director: "Quiero desarrollar una escena." [I wanted to unfold a scene.][14] His monologue frequently includes descriptions of Claudia as if she were being filmed: "Posa apoyada contra la puerta del automóvil." (p. 139) [She poses against the door of the car, p. 109] Mito's inclusion of himself in these imagined scenes indicates his propensity to enact his fantasies. For example, he notes his own astonishment: "Empiezo a girar, incrédulo, para asegurarme de que Claudia está allí y me cuenta estas cosas." (p. 144) [I begin to move around, incredulous, to assure myself that Claudia is there and telling me these things, p. 113] This slow turning has a staged, cinematic quality about it, as if he were in the camera's eye. These fantasies reach extremes that alter or preclude Mito's perceptions of what is happening around him.

Myth provides *Zona sagrada* with an appropriate context for developing characters by less traditional means. Most striking is the presence of Mito himself, whose psychological disorder makes him a counterpart to the mythical figure of Oedipus. The predictable structure of myth facilitates the awareness that clearly, this convention is subverted by Fuentes. It contextualizes the world of illusion, incorporating the explanation for inscrutable events typical of mythology, as a parallel to Mito's creation of an alternate reality.

The inclusion of a mythic dimension is appropriate to the novel's portrayal of alternate realities because of its permissive environment. It allows freedom from verisimilitude in its depiction of characters, as well as of temporal and spatial planes. The holy place to which the title refers is Mito's alone; Wendy Faris calls it his own "enchanted grotto." (p. 131) He controls its dimensions and determines what occurs within its borders. His apartment and his delusions about Claudia perpetuate the illusions he cherishes; they represent perhaps the only aspects of his life that function as he wishes. Mito's sense of control over this construct fulfills a need for the sense of predictability and stability that he is otherwise denied.

The mythic structure itself is subverted, however, as the narration declares its independence even from the mimesis of myth. Faris points out that this was foreshadowed in the opening scene of the novel. (p. 131) As they sit in a café on the beach, Mito and Giancarlo discuss an alternate ending to the myth of Ulysses, one that Gloria Durán identifies as loosely based on Robert Graves's reconstruction of the Ulysses myth.[15] According to the Graves version, Ulysses fathers two sons, one by Penelope (Telemachus) and the other by Circe (Teleodorus). Telemachus flees his home to escape the boredom of Ulysses' tales; on his adventures he becomes Circe's lover. Teleodorus eventually comes to Ulysses's home, kills him, and becomes Penelope's lover.

This alternate version establishes an important freedom in restructuring the myth as presented in Zona sagrada, and predisposes the reader to accept a structure that is different than expected. Mito as Telemachus is thwarted in his attempts to become his mother's lover, therefore he creates his own myth, a system of belief that rationalizes his mother's indifference, which is so painful for him. Giancarlo, as Teleodorus, is Mito's counterpart who eventually "gets the girl" and through whom Mito vicariously possesses his mother. His homosexuality and Mito's incest, moreover, move yet another step beyond the traditional, predictable order of myth.

The mythic and cinematographic contexts of Zona sagrada provide a vehicle for characterization as well as a rational explanation for the distortion of characters in the novel. Claudia probably began her career in cinema able to differentiate between her presence on- and offscreen. Now she has completely appropriated as her own the many roles she has interpreted in films; they allow her tremendous control over others, as she is conscious of the powers of the mind to make a screen image even larger than its larger-than-life image. Claudia acts according to the dictates of her self-perception; she molds herself to become what she envisions herself to be. Thus, her character never conforms itself permanently to a single mold. Always in motion, Claudia never truly "is" any of her roles.

Mito's obsessive viewing of Claudia's movies might have begun innocently enough, but this practice has produced a dark side that controls him. He cannot live outside the reality of the projected image that he has internalized and continues to project in his mind. Initially the screen is a means of approaching his mother; eventually it becomes the sole facilitator of his functioning.

The portrayal of the characters in *Zona sagrada* is based on the distortion of their own self-perception. The elements of myth and cinema provide a double vehicle in the novel, both as means of presentation of the characters, and as rationale for their eventual straying from the traditional figure of character: fragmented, always in motion, independent of external reality.

Equally significant to characterization in *Zona sagrada* is the psychological element. Guillermo's distortions in perception are due to his mental state, suffering delusions that place him on the verge of madness. Once this is understood, many of the changes that occur in the characters can be logically explained, even their patterns of continual transformation. It is possible to understand rationally Mito's Kafkaesque metamorphosis into a dog. Whether this is physical or mental, it is a real transformation in Mito's perception, one that is treated as if it were physically expressed.

The rupture of traditional sexual norms, as another manifestation of a crisis of identity, recurs in the novel's characters. Mito dresses up in his mother's clothing and, in his vivid imagination, sustains an incestuous relationship with her. Giancarlo is bisexual, and it is implied that Claudia engages in occasional lesbianism.[16] The oscillation between sexual identities contributes to the confusion between illusion and reality of Mito's world.

Claudia illustrates this conflict in somewhat different terms. Gloria Durán's study, *The Archetypes of Carlos Fuentes*, addresses Claudia's enormous power over others, a power that frequently proves destructive. (pp. 88–91) Durán labels Claudia a witch, capable of possessing others spiritually and of effecting total change. For instance, Durán shows that when Mito falls in love with Bella, a member of Claudia's harem, Claudia uses her body and soul to taunt Mito, destroying Bella's personality in the process.

This loss of an individual and determining identity is significant, particularly in the context of postmodern thought. Claudia's ability to enter into others through spiritual control presents not a coherent individual but a self that is separable, divisible into the two components of body and spirit. Mito and Bella's characterization points to the notion of a self that allows a removal or a shifting of its different components. The result is a self whose distinguishing characteristics are variable and subject to change. This conception of character carries weighty implications for the postmodern writer, as it points directly to a more accurate perception of the extratextual self.

While Claudia is the agent of change in other characters, she herself is susceptible to similar transformation. In his analysis of the characterization of Claudia, Jonathan Tittler points to the process of continual change that she undergoes. As she evolves into "all female roles through history, the 'real' substantive entity that we expect to be behind her different *facades* is never there." (p. 537) He terms her a "pure image in circulation," never settling down nor attaching itself to one permanent source. (p. 537)

This principle of constant transformation is fitting to the postmodern concept of character: characters are images of unfinished selves, still in the process of definition. It is implied that there is never a finished self, in the sense of a preterit or perfect entity. Rather, an individual's selfhood is redefined in terms of her increasing tolerance for irresolution within herself. The different components of selfhood, shifting continually, redefine the status of identity, and replace the notion of a whole and integrated self.

Fuentes anticipates this postmodern configuration of character in *Zona sagrada* in 1968, yet carries it to new extremes in *Cambio de piel*. Thus, he moves characterization towards postmodern conceptions in *Zona sagrada*, where the components of personhood are isolated and in continually shifting patterns, where sexual identity constantly changes and where projection and metamorphosis occur; however, these permutations of the notion of the self still remain within a mythic, cinematographic, and psychological framework, which offers a rational explanation for such transformation. *Zona sagrada* therefore remains a modernist novel, and it is not until *Terra Nostra* that fully postmodern expression, without the disclaimer of a rational explanation, is achieved in Carlos Fuentes's fiction.

As the novel of final transition between modernist and postmodernist fiction, *Cambio de piel* offers a wealth of pivotal junctures between both modes of presentation. The novel presents a similar treatment of epistemological perceptions of illusion and reality, although questions of an ontological nature begin to be addressed. The notion of the self becomes central to the novel's pursuits as its emphasis shifts from perceptions of the knowledge of reality to questions about being. The author constructs an artificial, fictionalized world wherein these questions are addressed at all levels of the text. The self-conscious fictionality of the novel anticipates postmodernism's overt treatment of all constructs (including fiction, art, and the self).

Fuentes refers to *Cambio de piel* as "una ficción total" [a complete fiction],[17] one that needs to be considered as such to understand its seemingly disparate and purposefully indeterminate qualities. The conclusion, repeatedly, in reading the work is that the writer intends to show that nothing is behind what we consider reality. He sets up characters, narrative stances, the text itself, only to demolish it later, to show it was all artifice.

Four tourists, Javier, Elizabeth, Franz, and Isabel travel from Mexico City to Veracruz. They spend one night on the way at a hotel and then visit a Cholula pyramid. The narration develops mostly internal tangents to their lives, weaving a complex tale that involves each character's search for identity and love. It is unclear whether Franz and Javier, who share Elizabeth and Isabel (Anglo and Hispanic halves, perhaps, of the same person) as lovers, are separate identities or doubles. The narration remains purposefully evasive on this point, making indecipherable the exact nature of each character and of the relationsips between them. The indeterminate aura of the text is explained on the last page, as the narrator is revealed to be Freddy Lambert, writing from an insane asylum. The previous pages could easily be dismissed as the delusions of a madman. In the meantime, however, the reader has been subjected to the difficulty of reading an exceedingly nontraditional text.

The dismemberment of the traditional text also occurs at every level of the narrative. The constant references to itself as fiction have an effect similar to that of watching a videotape of a surfing event. Suddenly a drop of water splashes the camera lens and viewers realize that they are separated from the wave by an artificial construct, in this case a video camera. Similar epiphanies occur often in the reading of *Cambio de piel*, as we are reminded constantly of the fictionalized status of the text.

The multiple contradictions present in the text also contribute to its dismantling. In their discussion of *Cambio de piel*, critics often resort to tentative terms to describe the novel even at the superficial level of the plot. For example, "The car breaks down or is sabotaged . . . a cave-in appears to kill Franz or Elizabeth."[18] At times events are left unclear, at others there are obvious contradictions. The conflicting endings are a prime example: either

Elizabeth and Franz are killed in an earthquake, and Javier later kills Isabel; or Elizabeth watches Franz die. Shirley A. Williams calls this "the ultimate exaggeration . . . a final parody of rhetorical technique and subversion of the mimetic principle."[19] Thus, the self-reflexivity of the text as well as the nonmimetic presentation of the characters' reality (that is, the creation of a world within fiction) serve to present alternate but simultaneous versions of reality.

The conventions of time and space are violated to yield an increased indeterminacy to the novel. The demolition of space is achieved through the gathering of the foursome in an ancient site of ritual—the pyramid of Cholula. Two historical times meet at this spatiotemporal juncture, as detailed in the novel's opening pages. Cortés's bloody conquest of Cholula in 1517 is juxtaposed with the travelers' visit to the ruins on 25 April 1964. In addition, the characters' reminiscence of past events flows into the present without differentiation, so that the linearity of time is lost, and simultaneity becomes the norm. As Bernard Fouques states, "Los tiempos y espacios barajables de la novela tienden a coincidir." [The novel's times and spaces can be shuffled and tend to coincide.][20] The effect of layering events from different time periods is described by Shirley A. Williams as that of a "sense of total futility of human history which fuses all times into one." (p. 116) In this postmodern view of history, the past is a subjective by-product of present considerations, as it is formed in the present time.

Intertextuality also contributes to the dissolution of boundaries. The references to movies, particularly, provide intertextual apertures that break open the space of the text. Elizabeth, for instance, bases much of the reconstruction of her life on old movies, projecting her own image into scenes with Humphrey Bogart. Her memories create additional levels of reality as she incorporates her past into a movie scene (or a movie scene into her past). This juxtaposition of representations of reality results in a memory she embraces as a true and accurate reflection of her past, replacing the actual events that brought on the memory. The narrator follows the same shift, as he constructs an entire scene around a fragment from a movie.

It is on the level of characterization, however, that the most extreme subversion of the traditional text occurs. The characters are of erratic form, often borrowing identities. It is no longer clear, as it was in Zona sagrada, who it is that undergoes transformation; shifting identities melt into each other in what Tittler describes as "a series of interchangeable options." (p. 587)

On the most literal level, the name-sharing of the protagonists serves to highlight their function as opposites, or as different aspects of each other. As Tittler states, "Isabel can be seen as a moment in Elizabeth's life; Elizabeth is what Isabel could become." (p. 587) Fuentes, too, has commented that "Isabel . . . es una repetición de Elizabeth a otro tiempo, a otro ritmo. Javier y Franz son dos rostros del mismo sueño" [Isabel . . . is a repetition of Elizabeth in another time, another rhythm. Javier and Franz are two faces of the same dream.][21]

The dual endings are appropriate, for they illustrate the bifurcation of possibilities for the narrative. Along with these instances of plurality, *Cambio de piel* indulges the exploration of a narrator who diversifies his role. Methods of characterization also illustrate a multiplicity of perspective. Characterization in the novel takes place on different levels, incorporating into characters elements from nontraditional sources (movies and puppets).

Bernard Fouques shows that the fragmentation of character is transferred to the narrative form. (p. 224) Having as its precedent the Boom, where form follows function, *Cambio de piel* illustrates the solitude and gradual decomposition of character identity in a narrative that shifts abruptly, truncated at every turn. Much of the text is reminiscent of the episode in *La muerte de Artemio Cruz*, between Artemio and his wife Catalina, where the verbal conversation is minimal and is juxtaposed on the written page with the internal turmoil of things they want but never say to each other. In *Cambio de piel*, the couple's fragmentation and alienation is further manifested in the narrative itself as it records their disjointed conversations, which often degenerate into what Shirley A. Williams terms "futile monologues or a 'duologue' between people who cannot hear one another." (p. 116)

Secondary characters, as well, contribute to this flexible text that seems eager to show itself as a fictional construct. The Monks in *Cambio* appear abruptly in the text as beatniks who are in Cholula at the same time as the protagonists. In his study of these characters, Fernando F. Salcedo states that their characterization is different since they are puppets, not characters.[22] They do in fact metamorphose into puppets, a parodic reflection of Javier, Elizabeth, Franz, and Isabel. The Monks also perform a parody of the narrator, as they control the puppets' strings.

The Monks function as a parodic representation of the narrator's creation of character. In the trial scene, the Monks are assigned a name, and with it a role, thereby acting as the embodiment of the primary characters. As they prepare to hold trial, they open Elizabeth's trunk and choose articles of clothing that serve as indicators of personality traits.[23] At times, the characters in *Cambio de piel* appear to adopt identities as easily as they don a change of clothes.

They impersonate the conflicting relationships between the protagonists as well as their individual turmoil. In the brothel, Elizabeth's Monk counterpart simulates giving birth to a miniature doll, thus dramatizing her frustrated motherhood. The Monks reflect the protagonists at another level as well: Javier, Elizabeth, Franz, and Isabel are trying to escape from their personal hauntings. Elizabeth suffers from a loss of love in her relationship with Javier and from a loss of identity, and resorts to making up her past from movies. Javier is pained by his failure as an artist. Franz carries the guilt of his past contribution to the Nazi effort as an architect, and Isabel has no past or future, only the present, due to her lack of identity. They seek a place where they can be free, and perhaps for this reason they travel. As Salcedo points out, the Monks also seek freedom, but it is a freedom from the narrator's control. (p. 78) This is significant because of the implication that the narrator has contributed in some manner to the characters' condition. If this could be changed, they could be more like they want to be.

The critical consensus of the narrative voice in *Cambio de piel* is that, contrary to a traditional role of complicity with the text, the narrator is belligerent and refuses to fulfill his prescribed role, leaving many connections to the reader. There is an inverse correspondence, then, between narrator and reader roles: as the first decreases, the second increases. As Jonathan Tittler shows, the traditional narrative role of storytelling is undermined as the narrator "becomes enmeshed in the narration on several different levels." (p. 587)

The narrator is revealed at the end to be Freddy Lambert, a patient at the Cholula insane asylum. He is a participant in the action, appearing early on in the novel as a taxi driver in Cholula who visits the ruins with the characters. He participates in the beatniks' parody, playing the role of judge in the trial. The narrator functions as a *persona* for the author, creating and destroying characters. Finally, his direct address to Elizabeth and to the reader amplifies his voice, and he insists on calling attention to his omniscient perspective; he makes it apparent that he knows Elizabeth's secrets, intimating that he and she were once lovers. The narrator's transgression of his prescribed role is one of many instances of breaking open the text to allow for the expression of its otherness.

This structure provides a precursor to subsequent narratorial manipulation in Fuentes's texts. The "narractor" of *Cabeza de la hidra* (1978) adopts several roles as character and as narrator; in *Una familia lejana* (1982), the narrator tricks the reader into becoming the responsible party in the continuation of the story, and in *Cristóbal Nonato* (1987), the narrator relinquishes control of several plot resolutions to the reader.

Zona sagrada and *Cambio de piel* include many elements that contribute to the development of a new phase of writing. In essence, there is an authorial loss of control, a carefully orchestrated loss wherein the traditional hallmarks of narration—chronology, authority, and identity—are gradually decimated or utterly transformed. The resulting fictions ardently advocate plurality not only of construction, but of reading, interpretation, and implication. The narrator's loss of control over the narration undermines his authoritative stance. He no longer is a generator of meaning but manipulates textual elements to produce only incessant activity. That the narrator directly addresses the reader is ironic; not only does he call attention to himself in his role as guide, but he deliberately misleads the reader so that his omniscience, as well as his trustworthiness, are seriously called into question.

The emphasis in *Cambio de piel*, particularly, on the process of writing is evidenced by its subversion of traditional forms of representation. The narrator's refusal to provide necessary clues for the coherence of the plot directly affects the reader's responsibility. The text becomes a meeting place for narrator and reader: having been placed traditionally on either side of the text, they are now forced to change places occasionally. Thus, the text is not a static product of a one-time creation, but an invigorated exchange taking place within the mind of every new reader. Her participation in this process of textual formation points to the ongoing process within each text, activated by individual readers.

On the level of characterization, this notion of an active text corresponds with figures who engage in constant transformation, whether willful or imposed. In Mito's case, the mythical context initially provides a route for his characterization, although it is repeatedly thwarted by Claudia's controlling influence. His eventual metamorphosis into a dog represents the extremes of change that occur in the novel. The question of whether Mito's transformation is physical or imagined is secondary. The fact that these changes are often internal facilitates their presence in novels that often operate on a symbolic plane.

In *Cambio de piel*, the development of the main characters takes place in part through the refraction that occurs twice. First Javier, Franz, Elizabeth, and Isabel are embodied by the Monks, then they are represented by puppets. Much of the novel centers on the conflictive relationship between characters. Characters frequently struggle with individuation as Javier does—he began as an artist and was incapable of fulfilling his calling. Other presentations of character result in an alternate version of the self, creating a text that is open to variance on many levels.

The authorial resignation of control, the loss of chronological framework, and the unraveling of the concept of character, no longer portrayed as an entity impervious to change, contribute to a flexible text. The reader acquires a greater role in lending coherence and causality to the narrative. We find that the possibilities of recombination of the different textual elements—that are as diverse as their readers—leave us with an open text, wherein plurality of interpretation is designed and expected. In addition to this, the text itself is always changing its skin, shifting the narrative stance and introducing characters that are unaccounted for in terms of origin and their placement within the text.

Thus, at every level of the narrative, the authority of the narrator, of time, causality, character, and text is subverted. The changing, palpably transforming nature of *Zona sagrada* and *Cambio de piel* creates fertile ground and rich possibilities for increased postmodern expression in Carlos Fuentes's later novels, beginning with *Terra Nostra*.

Terra Nostra (1975)

Reading *Terra Nostra* is like being at a carnival: although you might be standing in one place, you have the feeling that you are constantly moving. The reason is readily apparent: the plot takes place on two continents and chronicles events of almost three millennia. The narrative spans two generations but compresses the events surrounding the lives of three kings, historically. The number of figures that are involved in the scenes in Terra Nostra gives the impression of a constant parade of characters, with different identities or in several forms, figures who reappear at different junctures in the novel.[24] A closer look, however, reveals a structural and thematic presence that leads us to the conclusion that Terra Nostra is a postmodern text.

The subversion of any recognized, culturally legitimized construct guides much of the narrative. Chronological time and spatial planes take on an alternative presentation. The concept of character reaches new limits in this text where the permutation of figures is the norm, rather than the exception. The narrative stance shifts often to express the perspectives of several narrators.

These factors contribute to an aura of indeterminacy and uncertainty, creating a fiction through which the readers must often chart their own course, providing the necessary connections between identities, filtering historical inaccuracies that are presented as factual in this historical novel of sorts. They must differentiate between the multiple narrative voices; thus, theirs is an active participation. The text advocates plurality in its questioning of selfhood, in its obvious fictionality, and in its subversion of the authority of traditionally accepted constructs that assert their own applicability, to the exclusion of others.

The notion of plurality, inherent in Terra Nostra's form and theme, is illustrated by the novel's protagonist, Philip II. He is intent on building the Escorial as a memorial to his life, attempting to conserve for all time the essence of his kingdom, the embodiment of who he is. He desperately wants to be the last king in the Hapsburg line, and so control the destiny of the monarchy that he represents.

News of the discovery of a New World prompts great uncertainty in Philip II, as he comes to the realization that the world is not limited to what he knows. The intrusion of this new world is threatening to him because it shatters the boundaries of his worldview. Confronted with the fact of another reality of which he was previously unaware represents a loss of control, and nullifies his absolutist perspectives as it introduces new factors beyond his control. The New World is external to the principles he has spent his life upholding as King. Philip's authoritative version of reality is no longer adequate, and therefore not possible.

The proliferation of different aspects of the narrative underscores this premise. The character of Philip is a composite of the

Spanish Kings Ferdinand II, Charles I, and Philip II, as Margaret Sayers Peden points out.[25] The major events of the discovery of the New World that span many years are collapsed into Philip's lifetime. Columbus discovers America one hundred years late. These inaccuracies, flagrant deviations from historical data that are common knowledge, suggest that the alternate recording of fact is possible, and that the historical canon is not guaranteed to be unequivocal. Challenging the canon yields the effect of undermining a sealed notion of history, and advocates the admission of a plural history.

Terra Nostra poses as a historical novel, yet it displays a disregard for the notion of linear time. The narrative begins on the last day of 1999, then chronicles the sixteenth century reign of Philip II, and inserts an account taking place during Tiberius' rule. Skipping back and forth between these temporal frames creates the effect of simultaneity, suggesting that each historical setting occurs not in successive relationship, but on parallel levels of an overarching reality.

The manipulation of time contributes to characterization in the novel. Celestina, the character Fuentes appropriates from medieval Hispanic literature, appears youthful at different points in the novel, while other characters age around her. She explains that since she has sold her soul to the devil, her involvement with the spiritual realm, traditionally viewed as outside our temporal framework, facilitates her violation of linear time. Yet she eventually succumbs to our time and to the aging process. Sayers Peden calls her an integral part of the "central narrative line of Terra Nostra," as Celestina exists simultaneously as a woman and as a child, yet eventually becomes an "aged bawd."[26] Her movement throughout the novel illustrates the general patterns of the narrative in its subversion of a chronological concept of time. Through aging she momentarily submits to linearity, but she acts on her own timetable; not everyone conforms to it, as it is an individualized time. When she meets Jerónimo, after twenty years of separation, she appears the same as she did before; he, on the other hand, shows the effect of time. The implication is the existence of multiple possibilities of time, none of which reigns absolute.

This premise is supported by Fuentes's portrayal of the different conceptions of time that govern the New World. A blond youth washes up on a beach covered with black pearls, signalling his entry into a world where everything is new. He comes upon an ancient Indian sage, who directs him to the jungle, where he embarks on a pilgrimage. The old man explains to him the origins of the earth; the punishment of the gods in this legend is to remain upon the earth, "condenados a contar el tiempo de los hombres" [condemned to measure the time of man].[27] Fuentes places this version of time within an Indian context strongly reminiscent of the Aztecs. Although never mentioned by name, the associations with the Mexican Indians in the text are clear— the descriptions of men who arrive by sea and who are astounded to find other human beings and who are struck by the magnificence of the land. Fuentes thereby predisposes his reader to acknowledge the existence of a different temporal perception, within his or her own extratextual reality of the Indian worldview. The readers are led to hypothetical acknowledgement, at least, of the artificial nature of their own concept of time. It is neither universal nor absolute.

Fuentes's subversion of the absolute includes the notion of space. The text creates its own space, independent of verisimilitude. The manipulation of space follows a pattern similar to the treatment of historical data in *Terra Nostra*. The writer contextualizes a scene within a specific spatial plane, the shores of the New World, for instance. This hyperspace activates many images in the reader's mind: the vast richness of unexplored lands, curious and dangerous encounters with Indian peoples, Europeans' vulnerability in facing a world so different from their own.

Fuentes literalizes the imaginary in images that recall the New World chroniclers' attempts to describe the unfamiliar with a language that could not contain its diversity. What the reader then visualizes becomes the diegetic space in which the characters move, lending credibility to the created physical context. Fuentes thereby raises the status of fantastic scenes from imaginary to imaginable—from the epistemological to the ontological—in his creation of a reality that is not limited by the absence of a counterpart outside the text. The lushness of the jungle takes on enormous proportions and participates actively in the blond youth's pilgrimage. The scenes are not limited to exaggerations of what we know exists, but allow for a literalization of the effects of the physical surroundings on humankind.

The violation of traditional notions of space occurs on another level in *Terra Nostra*, as well, through intertextuality. One of the distinguishing features of the novel is its incorporation of a long list of fictional characters, borrowed mostly from Hispanic literature: Cortázar's Oliveira, García Márquez's Colonel Buendía, Guillermo Cabrera Infante's Cuba Venegas, Lezama Lima's Esteban and Sofía, Donoso's Humberto, Rojas's Celestina and Ludovico, Cervantes's Don Quijote, Zorrilla's Don Juan and Doña Inés, and Kafka's cockroach, for instance. Some characters are present only momentarily, others are incorporated into the narrative in what Walter Reed calls a "proliferation of stories."[28] Fuentes weaves these characters into a story all his own. We find, for instance, that Don Quijote's madness is explained by the extreme narcissism of his youth as the literary Don Juan. Literary time frames are tampered with since, in addition to this, Don Juan engaged in an affair with the young Celestina, a figure from the literature of Spain one hundred years before his time.

Other characters are introduced along with factual historical personages. In the novel, Philip II is also Celestina's lover. Through the creation of hyperspace, fiction and extratextual reality are superimposed, joined on the spatial plane of the text. Literature exists on its own level, thereby invalidating the absolutism of either fiction or reality. As Reed states, "The facts of history and the fictions of literature are finally kept apart only by the consensus of their readers . . . these opposing modes of discourse keep collapsing into one another." (p. 278)

Thus the concepts of history, time, and space that are inherent to traditional perceptions of reality are manipulated to expose their nature as constructs. They are presented as artificially imposed methods of perception that are useless when sought to be universally adopted. As the first step in becoming aware that any one construct may not be imposed upon a collective body, Fuentes advocates questioning the validity of constructs themselves. His postmodern use of other media in his text is of particular significance, as different paintings illustrate the thematic and formal concerns of *Terra Nostra*.[29]

Philip brings the Orvieto frescoes to the Escorial. Attributed historically to Lucas Signorelli, the novel has them painted by Fray Julián, a member of King Philip's court. As it is reflected in a mirror, one of these paintings mysteriously turns into another, an actual painting displayed today in the Prado, "The Garden of the Earthly Delights," by the Flemish artist, Hieronymus Bosch.

Both Signorelli and Bosch depict scenes from the Last Judgment, relying on what appear to be medieval norms and modes of expression. These images contain undertones of heretical implications, and Fuentes subverts them through shifts of perspective. Evelia Cavalheiro discusses the subversion from within of Signorelli's "Last Judgment": "The Orvieto painting, whose context is of a religious nature, is the pretext . . . that reveals the plurality of heterodoxy thought existing within the rigorous orthodoxy of Hapsburg Spain."[30] Lanin Gyurko calls the painting "a symbol of freedom on many levels, as it dramatizes heretics who defied the one, official dogma to explore alternative beliefs."[31] Thus, Fuentes utilizes intertextual references to painting to emphasize the truth of plurality over the certainty of a single interpretation.

The paintings in Terra Nostra serve another function as well, as a metaphor of the unique methods of characterization in the novel. Already we have seen how the paintings' dynamism reflects the continual movement and shifting patterns of the narrative. The violation of chronology also contributes to the aura of activity that surrounds the characters. The paintings' own transformations are the visual representation of the permutations of different sorts that the characters undergo continually. On one occasion, Philip looks at the Orvieto painting, and several of the figures turn and speak to him, independent of the stasis of the other figures in the painting. These inanimate images, painted on a canvas, come to life and become a part of the textual fiber, playing roles usually reserved for literary characters. As characters, they move about in the same plane, now equal members of the text.

As for the "flat" characters from other literatures, they too become flesh and blood within Terra Nostra's diegetic space. Celestina and Ludovico are the most obvious examples: they become central figures in the tapestry of the novel, much like those figures on the wall of the Escorial who step into the rounded plane of the text.

Extensive studies exist on the nature of character transformations in Terra Nostra.[32] These generally focus on changes in the form of reincarnation, doubling, fragmentation, and re-formation based on linkage with powers outside the self. It is significant that critics take for granted the fact of constant change affecting the characters. None of their studies, however, acknowledge this as a literary presentation of the threat to the notion of selfhood. The postmodern recognition of the implications of this presentation in literature for the condition of modern man provides an apt context for the constant permutation of textual figures. The three blond youths of Terra Nostra offer an illustration of this principle.

Catherine Swietlicki has characterized them as the psychological doubles of Philip, reincarnating the curse upon Tiberius, whose three sons would divide his kingdom. (p. 95) As she explains, they embody both the threat of plurality breaking the unity of an absolutist rule, and the separate components of Philip's personality. (p. 95) Although the three youths share the same physical properties—they are all blond with six toes on each foot and a cross on their backs—their functions are different. Cavalheiro states, "Once its destiny is fulfilled . . . [the painting's] forms disintegrate and dissolve to integrate another painting with different forms and colors." (p. 180) Like the pigments of a painting that combine to portray a total image, the blond youths as the "bobo," as Don Juan, and as the Pilgrim recombine to form the image of Philip, and of alternate possibilities to his life.

Many years later, in the New World, they find that the Bosch painting has been painted over with another. Each blond youth is reincarnated as another blond youth. (p. 97) This refraction of character creates the effect of a painting that is discovered to have another, original, underneath. The figure of Philip, central to the characters in the novel, is thereby symbolically extended. We find this process of character change to repeat itself throughout the pages of the novel.

The principle of constant change and its implied threat to traditional notions of personhood in the works of Carlos Fuentes begins with the characterization of Claudia and Mito in Zona sagrada. Claudia is a composite of the images of woman through time, and the text circulates the currency of her image. Mito, too, is continually undergoing transformation as his self-perception becomes increasingly unstable, deteriorating into the image of a dog. In Cambio de piel, the characters experience a double projection, first as Monks, then as puppets.

In Terra Nostra, the presentation of selves at simultaneous temporal junctures results in the effect of irremediable fragmentation. Each figure is incomplete, as its counterpart appears in a different space at the same time (Celestina and the three blond youths, for example). The self as an entity, then, is suspect in the novel. A postmodern reading suggests an alternate version of the self, approximated in Terra Nostra and further explored in later novels.

An alternative to traditional heterogeneous sexuality accompanies this presentation of selfhood. Philip II carries the courtly ideal of chaste love to an extreme, and never consummates his marriage. His wife, Isabel, by contrast, is a nymphomaniac, and in the course of events is Don Juan's lover. He in turn suffers from acute narcissistic tendencies and insecurities that drive him to insatiable promiscuity. The demented Queen mother is a necrophiliac and carries around her husband's decomposing body. Philip's father commits acts of bestiality with a wolf and Ludovico, Celestina, and Philip II engage in a *ménage à trois* in their youth. Thus, in *Terra Nostra* an alternative sexuality is the norm rather than the exception. The reader begins to expect the unexpected, much as it occurs in *Cambio de piel*. The admission of plurality implied by this nontraditional sexuality again depicts the theme of the novel and of postmodernity.

In the novel's final scene, Polo Febo and the newly reincarnated Celestina make love, and a hermaphrodite form results. The scene takes place on the eve of a new millennium; and the two characters are surrounded by apocalyptic destruction. Paris outside their room is burning, bodies lay mutilated in the streets, the Seine River is fetid with contamination. Implicit in the apocalypse is the possibility of a new beginning; death engenders life. Walter Reed labels the androgynous element of this last scene "a pluralistic reappropriation of body as well as earth." (p. 276) The hermaphrodite is capable within itself of engendering and conceiving a new life. Although the future is not determined in the novel, the possibility of renewal lies clearly at the end of the present reality.

The Old World had a chance at building a pluralistic kingdom when it discovered the New World, replete with difference and newness. The absolutism of its monarchs, however, led to a fatally narrow vision and condemned the possibilities of a New World to failure. On the last day of 1999, at the site of utter destruction, Fuentes presents an alternative, a third opportunity for Spain to recover. Given the nature of its mistakes, any different outcome precludes the abolition of an absolutist mentality and a willingness for tolerance. The conclusion of this matter is not in sight.

The novel thus ends openly, extending its implications for renewal beyond the closed cover of the text. The ending does not truly come to an end. The nearly eight hundred pages preceding it have chronicled massive quantities of possible versions for what is occurring, what has occurred, and what is to come. This deferral of conclusions is inherent to postmodern thought. Although the text is capable of shattering previous limits we have perceived and imposed on reality, postmodernism denies fiction the definitive statement that attempts in some manner to delimit or control.

The deferral of conclusive endings begins with *Zona sagrada*. As readers, we are unsure of Mito's transformation into a dog: is it real, or isn't it? As has been stated earlier, the implication is that it is a mental projection; thus it will continue indefinitely in Mito's mind. The bifurcation of endings in *Cambio de piel* also represents a deferral of endings: there is no conclusive evidence that clarifies which version of the characters' death is "true." Therefore, we can come to no conclusion about the most basic element of the text: the plot. In addition to this, the fact that the story is framed within another—inside Freddy Lambert's head—creates an expanse of alternative courses for the "real" story, the frame text.

A similar phenomenon occurs in *Una familia lejana*, where the narrator is revealed to be Carlos Fuentes. He is responsible for bringing to the readers the stories they have heard from Branly; now that they have heard them, it is their responsibility to carry on the transmission outside the text. So it extends infinitely, dispersed through the readers of the text. *La cabeza de la hidra* shares another similarity with *Terra Nostra*: it ends where it began. Circularity does not permit any ending to declare itself definitive. It is in *Terra Nostra* that Fuentes asserts this with such fervor that his subsequent fiction is irrevocably altered, and thereafter the novels begin with the awareness that they must not, and cannot, end.

Fuentes incorporates yet another construct in his monumental text in order to subvert the notion of a black-and-white world, governed by binaries. The number three becomes a structural device for the novel, breaking open the space left by the dissolution of binary opposition:

> "Uno es la raíz de todo. Dos es la negación de uno. Tres es la síntesis de uno y dos. Los contiene a ambos. Los equilibra. Anuncia la pluralidad que le sigue. . . . La corona del principio y el medio. La reunión de los tres tiempos."
>
> (533)
>
> [One is the root of all. Two is the negation of one. Three is the synthesis of one and two. Three contains both. It balances them. It announces the plurality that follows. . . . The diadem of the beginning and the middle. The reunion of the three times.]
>
> (526)

The novel's tripartite structure allows for an unexplored new ending. Philip's unrest at the question of the relativity of beginnings and endings is illustrated in the following incident: he waits to inaugurate the mausoleum to coincide with his birthday, so that others will not know whether to celebrate his birth or his death. He attempts to prolong his life and to attain immortality, hoping to indefinitely defer the ending of his life. Fuentes also depicts the third realm of life and death as memory, a conceit he further elaborates in all of his later novels.

Fuentes is most committed to not offering answers to the questions he poses. In postmodern fashion, he denies the absolute applicability of any one version of the truth, for as such it is only a construct, equal to any other and specific to a limited group. He engages the reader in a process of questioning as he exposes constructs as such. Terra Nostra may be considered a starting point, then, of Fuentes's challenging exposure of claims of the absolute.

Carlos Fuentes utilizes the space of his subsequent novels to continue the process of doubt. Moving from the epistemological concerns of his earlier novels to ontological ones, he uses innovations in the text to subvert the authority of constructs of time, space, identity, and reality (versus fiction) that have been championed as definitive. The fragments that remain of the notion of selfhood, particularly, admit to the condition of man, newly recognized as irremediable in its loss of identity. He includes a challenge of the constructed attempts of man to remedy his condition.

Fuentes dedicates his later novels, those written from 1978 forward, to expose this process. The texts see themselves for what they are, a narrative construct. The intertextual apertures, shifting narrative stance, and self-referentiality present in new form in Terra Nostra take a permanent place in Fuentes' fiction. Cristóbal Nonato and La cabeza de la hidra, particularly, redefine intertextuality in their postmodern incorporation of different media.

In essence, plurality of form and theme are advocated at every level of Fuentes's postmodern texts, beginning with Terra Nostra. The dynamism of this text must be attributed to more than its enormity of scope and great diversity of subject matter, readers, characters, and narrators. Fuentes subjects his readers to a loss of control over the text. Slowly he weans them from the text, reminding them that it is only another construct. Joel D. Black comments, "We are compelled to acknowledge further that all empirical reality is no less a fiction . . . for the reason that the very modality through which the world is experienced [ontology] and known [epistemology]—the matrix of space, time, and history—is itself more or less regulated through . . . discursive control."[33]

Of primary interest in studying the works of Carlos Fuentes is the nexus between reality and fiction. The presentation and interpretation of these two elements, whose area of convergence is the literary text, merit continued examination. In the matrix of his text, we explore with him the nature of all constructs, receiving the benefit of reading an ingenious text in which the questions addressed to fiction can be extended to reality.

Perhaps Fuentes's greatest achievement in *Terra Nostra* is to convince the reader that the process of questioning must go on. Having proposed to the reader the necessity of never settling comfortably within conclusions, Fuentes's own work is never done, and he continues his exploration of these issues in other fictions. Our reading of these texts perpetuates the process of challenging definitive claims, and so the endless proliferation of possibilities continues.

2

Reflections of a Narrator: *Una familia lejana* (1980)

Una familia lejana (1980) constructs a tale about story-telling, thereby making its subject the narrative process itself. As the novel's characters engage in story-telling, Fuentes elaborates on the act of narration, pinpointing its various components—the narrative agent, character, and reader—and challenging traditional assumptions regarding the mimetic function of literature.

The context of this metafictional commentary is one familiar to readers of Fuentes: it redistributes temporal and spatial conventions to create alternate realities; characters are molting figures who share identities, or function as doubles, or appear without ever being fully accounted for, leaving relations undefined and unresolved. The dynamics of relationship between the Old World and the New, played out by French and Mexican characters, treat issues of identity that are at the heart of cultural affiliation. The interaction of the past and the present is also of continued significance in Fuentes's 1980 text.

In the course of storytelling, the different narrators in *Una familia lejana* offer a variety of perspectives on one story, and also comment occasionally on the nature of the narrative act in which they are engaging. The self-reflexivity of the novel lends itself to an examination of Fuentes's own poetics of narration, and subsequently leads us to postmodern conceptualizations of the act of narration.

The story line revolves around Branly's encounter with the strange Heredias—Hugo, a Mexican archaeologist, and his son Víctor. Branly is a distinguished French count, eighty-three years old and a friend of the narrator's, to whom he tells the Heredias' story. Branly had previously met the Heredias at an archaeological site in Xochicalco, and when the pair visits France, Branly hosts them at his Parisian estate. In a game that the father and son invented and now play in foreign cities, they look in the local telephone book for others who share their family name. The Frenchman Víctor Heredia and his son André thus become involved in Branly's story.

Branly and the young Víctor remain at the French Heredias' mansion for a few days, recuperating from an automobile accident. A Gothic aura permeates the recounting of mysterious events that take place at the Clos des Renards. Their host is by turns gracious and condescending, almost cruel; the boys, Víctor and André, are inseparable playmates at first, then they are discovered engaged in sodomy, their relationship perverted by André's oppressive possessiveness that joins them in the irrevocable union of sexuality and, eventually, of death. Branly sees a white, ghostlike figure in a window and during his stay drifts in and out of dreams that recall specific incidents from his boyhood, and that repeatedly evoke the image of a woman he once loved.

In the course of the narration, as readers we come to the chilling revelation of the French Víctor Heredia's purposes: he seeks to perpetuate his own existence (later references indicate he is at least 160 years old) through another's memory. Having made a pact with the demonic Branly that enables him to prolong his life, he offers others access to the simultaneous, adjacent realm of death.[1] In exchange for transcendental proximity to loved ones who are deceased, others become mediums for Heredia's presence. Calling himself "un especialista en recuerdos" [a specialist in memories],[2] Victor Heredia approaches Hugo, who realizes that his memory of his recently deceased wife, Lucie, and son, Antonio, is quickly fading. Hugo rejects the offer, but his son, Víctor, accepts at the cost of his eventual death. Having become a medium, the young Víctor loses his autonomy as, inhabited by the presence of the Frenchman, he submits himself to his control. Víctor's fate is reminiscent of Félix's in *La cabeza de la hidra*: the domination of both characters' physical entities threatens their very identity.

The Heredia family phenomenon of access to the dead and to the past is secret, and the disclosure of the tale is punishable by the death of the narrator. The one who tells the story is eventually a victim of his own telling: he dies once the tale is repeated. When Hugo Heredia tells Branly this story, he transfers the weight of its silence onto the recipient. Branly feels the burden of this fated story, as it ends in the young Heredia's death, and he is compelled to transmit the story to the novel's narrator, revealed at the end to be Carlos Fuentes. Branly knows that his telling of the Heredia story will result in the death of Hugo Heredia, for telling the story causes the death of the previous narrator, as agent of the story's initial transmittal.

Here, the novel seems to inscribe the notion that the narrative process is a sequential transmission. Each previous narrator becomes contained within the story as it passes from one narrator to another. His death—or in Fuentes's novel, his assassination—comes from a subsequent telling of the story, leaving him fixed in a narrative text. All narrators eventually succumb to this fate as the story continues to be told. The narrator is saved from the damnation of being coded within a work only in texts that know themselves to be "an activity of production," in Roland Barthes's words.[3] Indeed, these too run the risk of becoming fixed, although their self-conscious activities postpone their narrators' demise.

Carlos Fuentes, in the final pages of the novel, is tormented by Heredia's ghost, and it is implied that he will tell the story in order to rid himself of such torment. Of course, the preceding pages have already transmitted the burdensome tale to us as readers; we are the next in line to keep the story's secret, but also to tell it, for each narrator exorcises the phantoms of narration only by telling the story.

In *Una familia lejana*, the act of narration is therefore fated to continue. The story maintains its power to ensnare its listeners so that they hear the whole story; once they have heard it, the story possesses them until it is transferred to another recipient by the act of repeated narration. Its curse of transmission guarantees that the story will be retold through the medium of unwilling narrators.

The reader of Fuentes's story is thereby implicated in the perpetuation of the narrative act. We discover at the end of the novel that Fuentes, the narrator, has ensnared us in his tale and we, like he sitting innocently before Branly, have been victimized by the power of the tale. The whole of this novel points eventually to the reader's participation in carrying on the narration, extending beyond the closed pages of the text. Fuentes, the writer, has executed a deft sleight-of-hand in entrapping his readers in Fuentes's, the narrator's, story. Presumably we as readers will heed the voice of the narrative phantom that beckons us to tell the story we have heard, and thus *Una familia lejana* might be extended to even further distant relations.

Here, then, the extratextual Fuentes continues the nonconclusiveness of novelistic endings initiated as early as *Cambio de piel* (1967). The last two words of that novel reveal that Freddy

Lambert, a patient in an insane asylum, is the narrator; this not only leads us to reconsider the veracity of the previous account, but allows us to see the expanse of alternate narratives that might follow this tardy revelation. Similarly, in *Terra Nostra* (1975), the beginning of a third millenium is hailed in the novel's final pages, marking a possible starting point for an adjacent manuscript that records the age to come. In *La cabeza de la hidra* (1978), the final repetition of the first scene displaces the novel's ending indefinitely.

Una familia lejana transfers the continuation of the narrative to its readers; they bear the responsibility for its survival. Fuentes pushes this notion even further in his later novel, *Cristóbal Nonato* (1987). Throughout Cristóbal's gestation, he addresses the reader outside the womb directly, thus forcing the reader into an actively participatory role. The acknowledgement of a reader, implicit in the earlier novel and included in specific references in the latter, functions similarly in the two novels: it recognizes textually the narrative variable of the recipient. Subscribing to the view that each reading is a re-creation of the text, Fuentes in his texts factors in the multiplicity of its readings. He thereby opens up the novel, once a monolithic entity, and so disrupts the predictability of reading.

Una familia lejana recapitulates the thematic emphases of Fuentes's novelistic corpus. The novel discusses the problematics of identity in cultural terms, pitting the Old World against the New. Branly embodies the aristocratic values of the proud European bourgeois; his sense of order is renewed simply by gazing on the manicured French gardens lying before him in perfect symmetry. Hugo Heredia, the Mexican archaeologist, searches for the wisdom of ancient times; the superimposed layers of obscured past civilizations have become his obsession. The novel is careful not to promote either culture above the other; rather, the duality is further complicated by the figure of the narrator, who feels his true self to be European, although he is Spanish American by birth. Although this issue never has a definitive resolution (to do so would be authoritative and therefore suspect), Fuentes problematizes its variegation and complexity. He does this primarily in the figures of both Víctor Heredias, whose assertions of cultural superiority—one Mexican, one French—can be attributed less to a strong sense of cultural identification than to their very lack of definition.

The past continues to exert its influence on the present, and most characters attempt, in one way or another, to regain access into the past. Branly, Hugo, and his son seek communion with a lost loved one; the French Heredia, though, seeks revenge for an incident that took place one hundred years prior to the time of the novel. Following individual motivations, the characters move through temporal zones adjacent or previous to the present, thereby discrediting the traditionally linear concept of time. As Fernando Burgos notes, the novel is an archaeological dig into the reverse side of chronology.[4] A sense of fluidity governs the characters' concept of time, as diverse temporal periods are juxtaposed, positioning previously sequential units in indeterminate constructions.

Prior to *Una familia lejana*, Fuentes had explored the simultaneity of the temporal in *Aura* (1962), *Cumpleaños* (1969), and *Terra Nostra*. In the latter novel, Celestina appears not to have aged while the bodies of others around her record the passing of time. Similarly, the French Heredia should be 160 years old. He exists in a separate but simultaneous realm that is ageless; he borrows mortal bodies only to gain access into their plane of reality.

The nonlinear conceptualization of time lends itself to Fuentes's portrayal of characters as figures who, as if incomplete and variable receptacles, frequently change their form. Their development is not regulated by a sequential ordering of events. In *Una familia lejana*, characters are beings who do not age, who can go back in time to a parallel reality and alter what happened in the past. Some make fleeting appearances, only to disappear without explanation. Therefore, causality is undermined as past and present, and the figures within them, mutually exert their influence on each other.

Through methods of characterization, Fuentes further explores the concept of selfhood. The shared name of Heredia provides an obvious lead into the doubling of characters. The Mexican is a younger version of the Frenchman—the young Víctor petulantly asserts his aristocratic upbringing using the same condescension with which Heredia flaunts his. It is probable also that André is a re-creation of his father, whose real name is also André. He is an expendable figure, as shown by his sudden and unexplained disappearance from the narrative. His absences seem of little consequence, since his father has secured the young Víctor as his medium instead.

Other forms of doubling occur in the novel as well. The notion of shared existences structures many of the figures; André and Víctor, for instance, form complementary halves of each other.

Their union is symbolized by two images: lovers engaging in sodomy, and two Siamese fetuses that the narrator finds floating in a pool at the close of the novel. The completeness of any union inevitably ends in death, as disparity, inconclusiveness, and contradiction form the essence of life.

Víctor's agreeing to serve as Heredia's medium opens his self to a shared existence. In addition, other figures throughout the novel facilitate another's remembering in less self-destructive ways. Branly, for instance, sees Víctor and André playing and remembers a childhood scene in which he failed to invite another boy into his circle of playmates. It is a painful memory, an omission that he regrets, and Branly sees André as potentially correcting it by reliving the past, this time including the child in his game. Branly, then, at least desires to share André's existence, coveting the opportunity of a second chance.

Some characters may shift external characteristics as they continue their existence through borrowed bodies. The maid becomes Lucie, Hugo Heredia's wife. Víctor/André Heredia possesses Branly, then Fuentes. Other characters in *Una familia lejana* disappear from the narrative, which is significant in that it implies the existence of another realm into which characters may slip, without the need for an explanation from the narrator. The reappearance of characters from the past—Lucie and the French Heredia, for instance—suggest the continued existence of characters who have been removed from the narrative context. Additionally, the French Heredia tells Hugo that he should look for his son in the countenance of a stranger. In effect, toward the end of the novel one of the waiters in the Automobile Club watches the narrator with light-colored eyes, a description that matches the initial depiction of the young Víctor's eyes: "Le parecieron azules y abiertos . . . verdes apenas los tocó la sombra de las gruesas pestañas." (p. 14) [They seemed so blue and dilated . . . green when his thick eyelashes shadowed them. (9)] Fuentes thus accounts for the transformation of one of his characters by referring to the supernatural realm of demonic possession, wherein one individual temporarily occupies the body of another, either adopting his features or changing them to resemble original ones.

The novel's portrayal of characters in a constant state of transformation acknowledges Fuentes's denial of the concept of the self as static. Not bound by temporal linearity, and thus capable of shifting into adjacent modes of being, the figures in *Una familia lejana* represent a fictionalization of the postmodern self.

The contemporary self necessarily remains always on the verge of change, as it is newly aware of the artificial nature of the units of time and is dismembered by the plurality of the culture that surrounds it.

The spatial element is similarly transformed in Fuentes's novel. There are numerous geometric references—to gardens, statues, majestic ruins, or buildings—that underscore the specific coordinates at which the narration is located. It is as though they provide the traditional Gothic enclosure for the mysterious series of events to take place. However, as Margaret Sayers Peden notes, "If once we could confine the nonnormal to a specific setting, a Gothic house, an enchanted wood, that privilege has been rescinded."[5] The inexplicable, the mysterious, and the supernatural expand from the Clos des Renards until they become the diegetic space of the novel. Thus, although the coordinates seem specific, they are in fact consistently unreal. The spatial element is mockingly precise, and progressively revealed to be a false construct of little objective value. Again, the hyperspace of the novel is definitively established as parallel to, not mimetic of, extratextual spatial contours.

Una familia lejana evokes specific locations, namely in France and Mexico; however, the frequent shifts between them contribute to a sense of movement and instability in the novel. The perfection of the French gardens conveys a particular fragility when they fail to transfer their artificial order onto the chaos of Branly's life. Even the ruins of the great Indian civilizations are only impoverished remains that archaeologists race to rescue from the wear of time. The solidity of the material world quickly erodes before us in the novel as it, too, falls victim to inevitable transformation.

However, in this novel's Proustian evocation of the past, objects become agents of memory in transporting a character to a distant past. An antique clock, a father's photograph, or the melody of a French madrigal fulfill this function in Una familia lejana. Placing a character within a recalled context, filling his senses with the remembrance of things past, these objects provide another avenue into adjacent realms of existence. Fuentes's evocation diverges from Proust's in that these forgotten times are not reversely chronological, but parallel. The novel, then, presents a fluid view of reality, allowing the nonlinear and irrational forces of undisclosed realms to exert their influence on the familiar conventions of reality.

In a parallel maneuver, the narrative structure of the novel aligns three versions of one story within the text, enriching the reader's perspective through a plurality of narrative accounts. Branly's encounters with Hugo Heredia become the basis of the story that he then relates to the narrator. His account is split by the insertion of another voice: within Branly's narration, Hugo is afforded the opportunity to give his own version of his meeting with the French Heredia. This constitutes Chapter 20; Hugo's presentation of his own story is preceded by Branly's comment: "Presentaré a Hugo Heredia como otro autor de esta narración." (p. 157) [I shall introduce Hugo Heredia as a second author of this narrative. (p. 163)] Hugo's narration is a subset of Branly's, and Fuentes, as narrator, tells a story that encompasses both versions. The narrative is therefore plural and collective, though still linear in its transmission.

Branly's storytelling takes place during several hours at the Automobile Club in Paris; he entices Fuentes by leaving loose ends within his story. The narrator is intrigued by Branly's story, and as he asks for clarification of gaps in his account, he becomes an accomplice in this narrative recreation of events. Branly reveals to the narrator that, now that he has heard Heredia's story, he is responsible for the transmission of the narration, as well as for Branly's own fate.

Fuentes is angry at having been trapped into the role of narrator:

No quería ser el que sabía, el último en saber, el que recibe el regalo del diablo y luego no sabe cómo deshacerse de él. No quería ser el que recibe y sabe para pasar el resto de su vida buscando otra víctima a la cual darle y hacerle saber. No quería ser el narrador.

(p. 190)

[I didn't want to be the one who knew, the last to know, the one who receives the devil's gift and then cannot rid himself of it. I didn't want to be the one who receives and then must spend the rest of his life seeking another victim to whom to give the gift, the knowing. I did not want to be the narrator.]

(p. 199)

The lugubrious tone of this section of the novel conveys the burden placed upon the narrator. As readers, we sympathize with the narrator's fate, until the realization that we of course are the next in line.

Delaying the revelation of the narrator's identity (Fuentes) until nearly the end of the novel serves to entrap us as readers into hearing the whole Heredia story. The burden of the narration is thereby transferred onto us. The author's perfect timing achieves a startled reaction from his readers who, immersed as we are in the tale, feel a momentary sense of panic at our forced involvement in the story. As we remind ourselves that this is just a fiction, we realize that this has perhaps been Fuentes's intent, as author, all along.

Una familia lejana is a work about fiction as much as it is a work of fiction. Fuentes's text resonates the concern, expressed by John Barth in 1967, of the burden of narratives that have preceded his own.[6] Both writers communicate the oppression of standing in the line of a vast legacy of literature, battling the impression that their progenitors have exhausted the possibilities of fiction. Yet their own fictions prove the continuing vitality of unexplored fictions. In his 1980 text, Fuentes problematizes the act of narration, and the often burdensome responsibility of narrating. Written on the heels of the extravagant *Terra Nostra*, the novel may be considered a postmodern rejection of the charge that contemporary literature is destined to mere repetition, not re-creation.[7]

In its portrayal of the burden of the narrative tradition that has come before it, *Una familia lejana* is acutely self-reflexive, as it necessarily exposes the dynamics of narration. In a conscious appropriation of the vehicle of interlocution, Branly tells the narrator that he will recall Hugo's voice through his own: "Escuche entonces mi voz narrar la de Heredia esa tarde de octubre en Xochicalco." (p. 156) ["Listen, then, through my voice, to Heredia's voice on that recent October afternoon in Xochicalco." (p. 162)] Branly thus exposes the traditionally invisible narrative medium: his voice will give the narrator access to words spoken in his absence.

Traditionally, the narrator's assertion of his presence at the scene of events lends credibility to his narration. In this novel, the narrator stands back and lets us see that his is a secondhand account. Branly is the central link in the transmission of the Heredia's story, and Fuentes makes no attempt to conceal this communicative debt. Of course, this serves the thematic purposes of the novel, providing a demonstration of the principle of inheritance, honoring the oral tradition of passing stories from one storyteller to another.

Hugo Heredia temporarily occupies the position of narrator. His account of meeting the French Heredia complements Branly's, offering additional explanation of the mystery surrounding this figure. Branly describes Hugo's status as "otro autor de esta narración," (p. 156) [a second author of this narrative, (p. 162)] in terms of a river flowing into this "carta hidrográfica que estamos dibujando." (p. 156) [hydrograph we have been tracing. (p. 162)] Branly's characterization of his story as a fluid entity, with neither identifiable sources nor known destination, constructs a metaphor for the act of narration itself. As different figures appropriate narrative expression, they create diverse versions of the fictional subject. These do not represent opposing truths, requiring the dismissal of one in favor of another; rather, they serve to illustrate the perpetual activity of narration, as "la naturaleza de lo narrado es que sea incompleto y sea contiguo." (p. 155) [It is the nature of narrative to be incomplete, to be contiguous with another story. (p. 161)]

As an underlying principle of *Una familia lejana*, this view of the textual process recalls Barthes's comments on the nature of the text. The inconclusiveness of narratives may be explained by the aim to remain as an aggregate, not a merging or a resolution, of disparate elements. The text is "not a co-existence of meanings but a passage, an overcrossing; thus it answers not to an interpretation, even a liberal one, but to an explosion, a dissemination." (p. 159)

Part of the incompleteness of the narrative act lies in its implicit charge to be passed on by the reader: Heredia tells Branly his story, who tells it to Fuentes, who tells it to the reader. The recipient of the narration is thereby involved, becoming an increasingly active participant in the textual process. The novel thus constructs an allegory of Barthes's refutation of the reading process as consumption of a text, asking of the reader a "practical collaboration" instead. (p. 163)

Una familia lejana anticipates the existence of its readership. As a postmodern text, it defies traditional downplaying of the reading process by drawing attention to the eventual, written quality of narration: "Dirá usted al leer esto. . . ." (p. 180) [You will say when you read this. (p. 188)] The novel serves the purposes of self-reflexive fiction by exposing the interlocutive vehicle and implicating the reader, in its aims to bring to light the very processes that guide its creation. This will be brought to fruition in *Cristóbal Nonato*, wherein the reader collaborates with the narrator in determining the outcome of the narrative.

Finally, Fuentes's novel challenges the notion of the mimetic function of literature. The foregrounding of the narrative processes places the text in the vulnerable position of having its methods reduced to a number of predictable constructs. In *Una familia lejana,* Fuentes creates additional barriers to perceiving fiction as an accurate reflection of life. He establishes early on the separation between living an event and telling about it:

> —Le he dicho que no podré entender esta historia hasta que termine de contarla.
> —¿A pesar de haberla vivido?, insistí.
> —A pesar de eso. ¿Qué relación puede haber, dígamelo usted, entre vivir algo y contar algo?
>
> (p. 139)
>
> ["As I told you, I shall not understand this story until I have finished telling it."
> "In spite of having lived it?" I persisted.
> "In spite of that. What possible relation can there be, tell me, between living something and telling it?"]
>
> (p. 144)

The narrative act is clearly distinct from life; therefore, its mimetic quality can neither be assured nor assumed.

In addition, Branly openly admits that a verbal account can only be an approximation of an event: "La imaginación narrativa . . . es capaz de reproducir algo verbalmente . . . así sea aproximativo. Esa proximidad incompleta será, de todos modos, la única verdad posible." (p. 157) [Narrative imagination . . . can reproduce a verbal account . . . [that] will be an approximation. In any case, that incomplete approximation will be the only possible truth. (p. 163)] He thus acknowledges both the inevitable distortion of events in narration, and the relativity of its differing versions.

In a variety of ways, the writer achieves, as a mark of a nonmimetic text, the subversion of sign correspondence. There are moments in *Una familia lejana* in which language experiences an occasional loss of its mimetic function. When Branly visits the Clos des Renards, the leaves are brown and fall from the trees, although it is summertime. This is similar to the linguistic breakdown of John Hawkes's *Travesty* (1976), wherein the dying trees are described as having bright green shoots.[8] In both works, the decomposition of language as a reliable and accurate conveyor of information conveys significant implications for the text as a verbal construct. It is Fuentes's intention to reveal the fragility of the narrative account by leaving this contradiction unresolved.

The element of coincidence structures many episodes in the novel. We have mentioned the Heredia name and the game with the telephone directory; the biographical data of the French Heredia bears an uncanny resemblance to the Heredia from Monterrey (also the result of the telephone directory) who approaches Hugo. In addition to their function as innuendos of parallel realities, these coincidences are too frequent to reflect reality. Conversely, the novel contains contradictions of fact that, although occasional and relatively unimportant, are disturbing because they are not assigned a final explanation. In her discussion of this aspect of the novel, Margaret Sayers Peden terms these contradictions a subversion of rationality. (p. 158) They effectively function, also, as subversive elements in the novel's campaign to discredit the veracity, and thus the authority, of the written account.

The aura of unreality that eventually extends beyond the boundaries of the Clos des Renards to permeate the entirety of the narrative scene further underscores the nonmimetic purposes of the novel. The representation of time and space display the most obvious aberrations; the figures who people this account are also revealed to represent strange possibilities of existence. The unreal is not confined to a place apart from our own; it cannot be reduced to a specific location. Rather, it is portrayed as a generalized condition. Therefore, if one is to accept the portrayal of reality in *Una familia lejana* as mimetic, the implications for the configuration of the reader's reality are overwhelming. At some point, the reader is forced to discredit either the novel's traditional claim to mimesis, or her own perception of reality.

Paradoxically, Fuentes's novel blurs the distinction between the fictional and the real. When the reader is charged with the responsibility to tell the story she has just read, she is compelled to provide it a point of entry into the "real", extratextual world. This poses a problem for literature that lays claim to mimetic representation, for the tables are turned. No longer does literature merely reflect life; literature is now granted a creative role, as it aspires to direct events external to the fictional world. Fuentes narrativizes this directive status in *Una familia lejana*, as readers are manipulated to continue telling the story they have just read.

The incorporation of other narratives within a text brings them to life, so to speak, as it resuscitates words on a page in their interaction with a new textual entity. The narration's power of evocation is reenacted in later texts, creating an interdependence that lends vitality to the realm of literature. As it cuts across other texts, intertextuality makes literature, not life, the referent of the current text-in-progress. For instance, Jules Superveille's poem, "La chambre voisine," appears as an epigraph to various chapters; Sayers Peden demonstrates its contribution to the structuring of the novel itself. (pp. 165–68) These epigraphs are not simply a passing reference to another work; rather, Fuentes weaves the poem into the very fiber of his narrative. It lends the novel a firm grounding in a preexisting literary model, as much as the novel's prose fleshes out the poem's condensed narration.

Fuentes first radicalizes the notion of intertextuality in *Terra Nostra* so that, unmistakably and extensively, he incorporates other texts along with actual historical personages. *Una familia lejana*, in its acknowledgement of indebtedness to other texts, goes so far as to list the works of fiction that are included in the text. (p. 198) Once again, Fuentes narrativizes in this novel a practice inherent to the composing of fiction. To date, he continues to weave a clearly intertextual fabric in his texts.

It is evident, then, that intertextual references gain particular significance in the self-conscious novel. These allusions to parallel works of literature are conspicuous reminders of the constructed nature of fiction. Texts are conceived as recombinations of other narratives, not as faithful re-creations of life experiences.

Through Fuentes's inclusion of himself in the text, he further parodies the notion of textual proximity to life. He challenges the traditional assumption that the narrator is in fact the author, the physical entity that writes the published page. Narrativizing Roland Barthes's description of the text upon the death of the Author, Fuentes inscribes himself in the novel:

> Like one of his characters, figured in the carpet; no longer privileged
> ... his inscription is ludic. He becomes, as it were, a paper-author:
> his life is no longer the origin of his fictions but a fiction contributing
> to his work.
>
> (p. 161)

Una familia lejana, then, may be considered a companion text to all of Fuentes's postmodern fiction to 1993, articulating his conceptualization of narrative expression. Indeed, Fuentes admits to being partial to this novel, because it "allowed him to perceive the unity and the incomplete, unbalanced nature of his own work."[9] The novel's self-reflexivity may be explained by Fuentes's experience in writing the novel, as it clarified his own poetics, defining his literary methodology and goals.

In this text, Fuentes exposes the traditionally invisible medium of interlocution, as different narrators consciously appropriate the narrative voice. The reader is positioned to become inextricably involved in the narrative. The nonmimetic character of the narrative presents alternate realities, such as simultaneous time and shared existence. The plurality of narrative voices implies a non-unity, a refraction of univocal authority and therefore a negation of absolute Truth. In the end, *Una familia lejana* stands incomplete and contiguous to other stories, conveying a sense of indeterminacy about life, as well as about the recording of life.

The result is one of marked textual plurality. The novel begs to be reread because it is not conclusive; perhaps a second reading will lead the reader to a different sense of its components. The effect is similar to that of *La campaña* (1990), whose final revelations of authorship undermine the narrative perspective that has guided the entirety of the novel. Thus, the novel calls for a fresh, meticulous reading that expands the possibilities for alternate interpretations.

Continuing alternatives for the narration are also implied in the reader's newly acquired storytelling responsibility. As the story is retold, its transformation is unavoidable and, by its becoming new, kills off the old. The novel anticipates *Gringo viejo* (1985), as Harriet practices this retelling of forgotten stories. She will resuscitate both Arroyo and the Old Gringo through memory, which recreates their story at the moment of each evocation.

Finally, the plurality of *Una familia lejana* is evident in the exploration of new realities that will come as a consequence of the narration's freedom from traditional mimetic guidelines. Fuentes's *Cristóbal Nonato* (1987) best illustrates this possibility for nonmimetic fiction. Positioning the narrative from a fetus's point of view, the writer sets his story in a future Mexico that is neither distant nor improbable. In spite of its ludic quality, the novel succeeds in its satirical intent, its succinct and thoughtful views taking rigorously accurate shape as the reader considers the conditions of contemporary Mexico.

Fuentes's poetics of narration, as expressed in *Una familia lejana*, represent a compendium of his postmodern aims as a writer. Although his most recent narratives are best understood within this context, they also continue Fuentes's purposes that have been clear from the beginning of his career. The primacy of language as a creative force is accompanied by the artist's acute perception of his world; therefore it depicts, albeit nonmimetically, possible configurations of reality. Fuentes's representation of the self, for example, as an unfinished entity depicts his perception of the indeterminacy of his contemporary world. The later stages of his novelistic production, particularly since *Terra Nostra*, represent a radicalization of these concepts. Perhaps Fuentes himself best summarizes his narrative intent, evidenced by his most recent works:

> La novela refleja, a la vez que crea, un mundo inconcluso hecho por hombres y mujeres inacabados también: ni el mundo ni los individuos han dicho la última palabra. La novela potencial es el anuncio y la garantía de una historia potencial: de una vida potencial, de la presencia potencial humana inacabada expresándose mediante el lenguaje narrado.[10]
> [The novel reflects, while it creates, an unfinished world made by men and women unfinished as well: neither the world nor the individuals have declared the final word. The potential novel is the herald and the guarantee of a potential history: of a potential life, of the potential, unfinished human presence expressing itself through narrated language.]

This statement characterizes Fuentes's novelistic production from 1975 to 1991 in particular. It reflects the postmodern view that holds the text and the self in indeterminate suspension, never final nor complete. The text is therefore to be viewed, above all, as a record of textual activity, and not as its product. As a narration about storytelling, *Una familia lejana* provides us as readers a guide to his post-*Terra Nostra* texts, each of which records a chosen manifestation of narrative activity.

3

Crises of Identity: Text and the Self in
La cabeza de la hidra (1978)

*L*A CABEZA DE LA HIDRA (1978) MAKES ITS APPEARANCE THREE YEARS
after the publication of *Terra Nostra*, and the difference in the
texts is striking. The latter is a historical novel nearly eight hundred pages in length, the former is a spy thriller less than three
hundred pages long; the action of one crosses continents and
covers a period of two thousand years, the other takes place primarily in contemporary Mexico City and narrates the events of
three weeks' time; *Terra Nostra* is encyclopedic in scope and
amasses vast historical and literary references, whereas *La cabeza de la hidra* follows one, albeit complex, story line encased
in the narrative trappings of the detective genre.

These apparent differences, however, thinly veil issues significant to both texts that respond to postmodern considerations.
Terra Nostra's exploration of the problematics of identity, treated
in Felipe's character, are enlarged to become the focus of *La
cabeza de la hidra*. The postmodern view of the self is illustrated
through the denial of individuation of the protagonist, whereby
a series of events causes irrevocable transformation and loss of
control. The protagonist loses his sense of self, resigns himself
to external forces and, his old self in shambles, adopts an entirely
new identity.

This crisis of identity extends to the text, as Fuentes utilizes a
genre that he not only exploits but subverts to call into question
issues of narrative authority and control. He experiments with
narratorial stance and roles, utilizing the conventions of the spy
genre to underscore his postmodern views regarding narrative
undermining and textual autonomy.

In its presentation of the protagonist and of his country, *La
cabeza de la hidra* draws parallels between the process of individuation at the individual and at national levels. Written in
1978, the novel comes on the heels of a global oil crisis and

may be considered yet another warning by Fuentes against the reduction of Mexico's territory. A frequent subject of his writing, the dangers of interventionism are further illustrated in his later novel, *Cristóbal Nonato* (1987). This novel depicts an image of Mexico in 1992, carrying the circumstances surrounding Félix's involvement in the spy network to their full implications. *La cabeza de la hidra* thus explores crises of identity at the individual and textual levels, and foregrounds issues of a collective nature that are central to the subsequent novel.

Félix Maldonado, the protagonist of *La cabeza de la hidra*, is a rather typical Mexican bureaucrat who becomes involved in the intrigues of a web of spies representing foreign interests in Mexico's vast petroleum reserves. The novel centers on Félix's struggle for individuation—the process by which an individual differentiates her or himself from others and acquires her or his own sense of identity—that for Félix is constantly subverted.

Félix's crisis of identity results from the imposition of external control that manifests itself in a loss of freedom and of his rights as an individual, and in the extensive transformation of every aspect of his life. He is framed as an assassin, then kidnapped; he undergoes plastic surgery against his will; he is stripped of his job, his name, and his wife; and he is strong-armed to assume a new name and identity, that of Diego Velázquez. His is coincidentally the name of the Spanish painter to whom Félix bears an uncanny resemblance. Félix's involvement with the budding nationalistic spy ring begins two years prior to the action of the novel. Timón, head of the spy ring and narrator, draws on their past acquaintance as roommates at Columbia University and approaches Félix with the intent of using him as a front to lure the enemy and lead Timón to their headquarters. Félix initially consents to a peripheral role but quickly loses autonomy when he is forced by the Arab enemy, led by the sinister Director General, to act as their own front. The complexity of the intrigue intensifies once Félix becomes a double agent, as he begins to see himself a victim of overwhelming and conflicting forces.

Both the narrator and the Director General are in search of a ring whose stone contains holograms of the size and location of Mexico's oil reserves. The projected images resemble a hydra head and, in the hands of foreign forces, they could jeopardize the Mexican oil industry's future. The ring, produced by Bernstein, the Israeli agent, is on its way to the United States, and three groups—the Arabs, the Israelis (who cooperate with the CIA), and the Mexicans—are in search of the ring. In the course of the search for the ring, Sara Klein, Félix's great idealized love from his youth, is murdered. Once he recovers the ring, Félix resolves to avenge Sara's death; thus, he becomes even more deeply enmeshed in the underworld of spying activity.

The central symbol of the hydra applies to thematic, structural, and technical aspects of the novel. The spontaneously regenerative nature of the hydra is paralleled in the text in what Lanin Gyurko calls a "recurring emphasis on duality."[1] The doubling occurs in scenes (the first and last are nearly identical), in characters (the genre's tradition of double agents and disguise provides a convenient vehicle), and finally, in the fate that is shared by both the protagonist and his country. Gyurko discusses the eventual consequences of this incessant doubling: "At first seeming to attest to the expansion or to the transcendence of the identity, or to its self-renewal, the double finally attests to a loss of control—the inability of either the individual or the nation to determine its identity." (p. 262) Félix's fragility and vulnerability to external domination are mirrored and magnified in the novel's depiction of Mexico at the hand of greedy foreign investors. The reader witnesses the final outcome of the individual's situation, and this infers the plight of the entire nation. It is not until *Cristóbal Nonato* that Fuentes actually paints the scene as he imagines it in *La cabeza de la hidra*.

The principle of proliferation of the narrative elements described above is fundamental to the understanding of *La cabeza de la hidra*. As Gyurko concludes in his study, the principle of duplication is inherent in the narration at the level of narrative structure, character, and thematic concerns.[2] Acknowledging the accuracy of his observations, this discussion will propose further conclusions as to the significance of this principle, particularly within the context of postmodern thought.

Timón initially approaches Félix armed with an arsenal of manipulative techniques. He plays on Félix's passionate loyalty to President Cárdenas for his nationalization of the oil industry. Félix had grown up hearing that Cárdenas made it possible for the Mexicans to look foreign oil owners in the face; he recounts his father's perception that he and other previously faceless employees began to have individually distinct countenances. The novel thus links the act of regaining ownership of oil to the legitimation of Mexican identity. The symbol of facelessness as lack of identity is central to the novel, as masks and disguises serve to substitute or to cover identities. Félix's facial surgery represents the physical evidence of the power others wield at the expense of his sense of self.

Félix's susceptibility to Timón's manipulation is compounded by his pre-existing instability, as discussed by both Lanin Gyurko and Philip Koldewyn. Gyurko states, "The original identity is . . . weak and unstable. At first Félix appears as a person with little or no inner self . . . that changes constantly because it has no true center." (p. 243) The result is a proliferation of alteration that, much like the hydra, is continually changing its shape in fluid movement and in the growth of replacement limbs. These changes are represented in Félix's evolution through different roles, each of which brings its own series of transformations. Félix is first a savior, agreeing to serve as a front to protect Mexican interests. He becomes a victim when he is forced to change his looks and his livelihood; then he is an aggressor, defying Timón's instructions by taking vengeance for Sara's death into his own hands. He is subsequently a victim again, utterly powerless in the face of newly imposed control. The novel ends with a defeated Félix: he assumes the identity of Velázquez, an invention of the Director General's, and he is submitted to a circular pattern of domination.

The imposed transformations critically threaten Félix's self-perceptions and prevent him from ever achieving wholeness. The novelist succeeds in his portrayal of a character who succumbs to this fated unraveling of a sense of self through the conventions of narrative plotting. Félix's identity is crisscrossed by two plots, primarily, that are forced upon him. First, as a spying agent, Félix submits to playing a variety of roles, as Timón's lure and as the Director General's pawn. He undergoes physical transformation to enhance his role as a spy chasing after the hydra ring. Secondly, as the platonic lover of an idealized Sara Klein, his plotted course of action follows the conventions of chivalry. Félix is thus compelled to avenge his ladylove's death. This second plot runs contrary to the first, as fulfilling his amorous duty sidetracks Félix from following Timón's and the Director General's orders. It is Félix who bears the emotional duress caused by these conflicts of interest. The contradictions of these plots further fragment Félix's sense of autonomy.

The imposition of roles on Félix is successful to this extent only due to his preexisting weakness. Koldewyn describes Félix as "un hombre cada vez más dividido e inseguro de su identidad" [a man increasingly divided and insecure of his identity].[3] He attributes Félix's fragmentation and crisis of identity to the psychic split between eros and logos, which he argues is a fundamental principle of the novel. This appears to be accurate, in light of the fact that Félix's actions are limited to acting out the conventions of plot. Gyurko also demonstrates the principle of colonial domination at work in the novel, as Félix's tormentors destroy his confidence about his identity. This is reflected on the national scope in the case of Mexican oil which, in spite of its nationalization in 1939, still serves foreign interests, and thus continues colonial patterns.

Gyurko cites an incident from the Conquest, wherein young Indian prisoners of war were branded on the face with the letter "G."[4] As its novelistic counterpart, Félix's surgery results in his acceptance of the new identity imposed on him, for he becomes convinced that he has been irrevocably transformed. Even before the surgery, people he has worked with for years pretend not to recognize him; after his surgery, he is certain that he is unrecognizable. But Bernstein, his university professor and long-time friend, recognizes him and says, "Tu única cirugía es la de la sugestión." [The only surgery that was performed on you was that of suggestion][5] Félix Maldonado is swayed by the power of suggestion because of the absence of a defined sense of self.

As evidence of Félix's impoverished sense of self, the text provides several instances of Félix's assimilation of traditionally non-Mexican lifestyles. Félix converted to Judaism when he married Ruth, although he does not practice this religion. He breakfasts at Sanborn's and orders waffles and syrup, while his companion orders the typical Mexican "huevos rancheros." He drives a Chevrolet and seldom walks downtown. On those rare occasions, he crosses the street to avoid having to look at beggars, and once comments that Mexico's streets are unfit for gentlemen to walk on.

Félix's sense of identity is further problematized by a denial of his Mexicanness. His specific rejection of those elements of society of which he does not consider himself a part is a reminder to Félix of his Indian past, which he rejects. A constant in Fuentes's novels, this type of character denies this vital component of his past and never fully achieves wholeness as an individual; his identity is always incomplete. With this in mind, one can better understand the extent of transformation to which Félix succumbs during the course of the novel.

Félix's lack of internal coherence predisposes him to adapt to the new face, role, name, and profession—in short, to the new identity that is forced upon him. His crisis of identity is initially

brought on by self-doubts that plague him. Early references point
out his striking resemblance to the seventeenth-century Spanish
painter, Diego Velázquez, and he is threatened by the fact that
he looks like someone else. Ruth consoles him by saying, "No,
Velázquez es tu doble." (p. 39) [No, Velázquez is your double.
(p. 35)] It is ironic that the new name assigned him is Diego
Velázquez.[6]

When Félix awakes from the surgery, he finds himself wrapped
up like a mummy, unable to speak. With him in the hospital
room are the Director General and his henchman, Simón Ayub,
modeled after the actor Peter Lorre.[7] They tell Félix that he has
been accused of attempting to assassinate the Mexican President;
the news reports that Félix was imprisoned, then shot upon trying to escape. His funeral services were held the next day.

Félix is unable to express his anguish, but feels the fingers of
control tightening around his neck: "Admitió pasivamente que
era algo peor que un prisionero de estos dos hombres: era una
lombriz con la que jugaban cruelmente, cortándola en pedacitos,
picándola con una vara para ver si seguía moviéndose." (p. 68)
[Felix . . . admitted passively that he was worse than a prisoner;
he was a worm they were toying with cruelly, cutting into little
pieces, and prodding to see if it still moved. (p. 67)] The Director
General reminds Félix that at least he is alive, and only because
all they want from him is his name, to assign as the culprit of
the assassination attempt. The Director General's plan to separate
Félix's name from his identity is part of his brainwashing to
which Félix, as an already fragmented individual, is particularly susceptible.

The Director General's mounting control over Félix balances
Félix's diminishing control. From the time of his first meeting
with Félix, who can't open the door to leave because it is controlled mechanically from the desk, the Director General system-
atically appropriates Félix's rights to speech, individuality, and
freedom of choice. He not only undermines Félix's plans, but
widens his influence to supersede even the script that the narrator had proposed for Félix. One controlling mechanism replaces
another and what begins, then, as an internal lack of coherence
becomes permanent instability for Félix, the result of an identity
that is forged from the outside. Félix does not sustain an essential
core of self through these transformations; he is entirely at the
mercy of plots that are forced upon him.

A reassessment of Félix's initial characterization thus becomes
necessary, and a third plot is soon apparent. As an automaton

of bureaucracy, Félix dutifully abides by its conventions—the starched formality of his dealings at the office; business breakfasts; a wife from his social class; a conservative plan that chooses to wait to have children until their future is economically secure; and maintaining a hotel room, as well as an apartment, for business purposes. We then come to the conclusion that Félix did not, in fact, start out with a sustaining core of identity, nor does he become anchored to one at any point in the novel. The novel's circular ending implies that his destiny, as an individual that has been denied the process of individuation, is doomed as well.

The parallels between Félix's plight as an individual and his country's at the hands of foreigners—first, gold- and fame-seeking during the Conquest and now oil-greedy—are clearly delineated in La cabeza de la hidra. Lanin Gyurko points out the frequent instances in which issues of a national scope resonate in the text. He states that the novel reduces the Mexican plight to the size of an individual, Félix Maldonado; conversely, our conclusions about the consequences of Félix's unstable identity can also be applied to the nation as a whole. As Gyurko notes:

> In La cabeza de la hidra, Fuentes demonstrates the great extent to which the individual, in this case the hapless bureaucrat Félix Maldonado and, on the symbolic level, the Mexican nation, are under the control of external forces that manipulate, exploit, and finally have the potential to destroy them. In the case of Félix, this destruction is completed. In the case of Mexico, Fuentes stresses the ease with which his country becomes a pawn of the superpowers.[8]

By the end of the novel, Félix is at a loss to identify who controls his life and, in a broader sense, realizes he is incapable of knowing under whose control the rest of the world operates. The Director General dismisses Félix's indignation over their usurpation of his identity; he is annoyed that Félix could still think that was important, and his reaction is like that of an Egyptian priest, "ultrajado por la presencia de un monoteísta." (p. 68) [affronted by the presence of a monotheist. (p. 67)]

The conclusions implicit in the text regarding identity and control have clearly postmodern overtones. If the individual is wholly defined by external forces, then no core self remains. These forces are variable to such an extent, and so frequently exert their influence, that the self is necessarily pluralistic and subject to change. No longer a fixed essence, insulated from ex-

ternal influence and capable of remaining unchanged, the self is
more of a flexible receptacle of roles, names, faces, and re-
sponses. No center holds these elements in place; even though
differentiating characteristics might temporarily be suspended
in a holding pattern, giving the impression of definition through
individuation, this is only a fleeting illusion. The self can only
define itself in relation to others, not on an absolute scale, and as
different elements come into its orbit, it is destined to perpetual
transformation.

Félix is not the only character who suffers from a crisis of
identity. The narrator of *La cabeza de la hidra* also lacks the
certainty of knowing who he is, and is a little unsure of who
pulls the strings that control him. The narrative voice is refracted
into the first and third person; through most of the novel, Timón
gives a detached, third-person account of Félix's activities, but
occasionally inserts first-person commentary as Félix's master
spy who directs his activities. This near-schizophrenia may be
explained by the narrator's apparent indecision as to his role in
the text: is he character, narrator, or scriptwriter?

The narrator's identity is cloaked in secrecy—appropriately
enough, considering Fuentes's choice of the spy genre in *La cabeza de la hidra*. We are never told the narrator's real name, as
Félix calls him only by his code name, Timón. Timón first gives
Félix orders in the Nineteenth of forty-nine chapters. However,
it is not until Chapter Forty-One that the narrator reveals himself
to have played the part of Trevor, a triple agent with whom Félix
had contact earlier in the novel. Timón's self-perception of his
roles in *La cabeza de la hidra* is multiple: as a scriptwriter of
the events revolving around his spy ring, he orchestrates the activities of that ring; he includes himself as a character posing as
a triple agent. Finally, as his name indicates, Timón views himself as the rudder controlling the direction of the narration. Timón merges these roles and leaves a chartable course to his
failure to maintain control both as scriptwriter and character. He
is reduced to playing the role of narrator, stripped of control.
Through Timón's delusions of control, what is ultimately at stake
in the novel is the undermining of narrative authority.

As Trevor, his professed allegiance to Arab and Israeli interests
masks his double betrayal when he apparently acts in the interests of his own Mexican organization. However, what Timón presents as national interests are clearly his own: he seeks to protect
his family's petrochemical manufacturing business. Toward the

end of the novel, these and other signs begin to reveal cracks in Timón's carefully lacquered exterior.

A master of disguises, the narrator, as the double agent Trevor/ Mann, manages to hide his identity from Félix, his graduate-school roommate for two years. Throughout his life, the narrator has made use of disguises and role-playing (he mentions once that he and his sister obsessively played dress-up as children). This practice has encroached upon Timón's adult life: even when he speaks with Félix, he wears a false moustache. When he takes it off alone in his room, it is carefully placed in one of the many boxes containing other means of disguise—wigs, false eyelashes, sideburns. His closet is full of clothing from all over the world, which he uses to reinforce the different regional accents and languages he adopts when playing a character. As he removes the false moustache, it sticks to the new one underneath, but perhaps that, too, is counterfeit. The narrator slips from one *persona* to another all too easily, thereby effectively illustrating how shallow his identity is, how elusive is his real self. The reader thus attributes the narrator's eventual failure to control the narrative to his incapacity to control himself.

In the scene previous to the one described above, Timón makes sexual advances towards Félix, which Félix rejects. Gyurko interprets the scene as Timón's attempt to substitute professional control with personal domination,[9] as Félix has made clear his intentions to avenge Sara's death, regardless of Timón's plans. Although this might be mistakenly interpreted as Félix's assertion of his rights, he is instead slavishly responding to the conventions of a plot that has been imposed upon him.

Following this encounter with Timón, Félix loses his temper, angry that he has risked his life repeatedly while Timón sits at home. They wrestle in a struggle for domination in which they are evenly paired. Timón, however, considers himself defeated, because he has not succeeded in dominating Félix. In his previous roles, wherein he has merged his narratorial status and his power as Félix's boss, he has been accustomed to total domination. Finding himself evenly matched with Félix, he perceives equal status as defeat. Thus, when he returns to his room and removes his moustache, the reader gains insight into the narrator's own perceived vulnerability, especially as he climbs into his "cama sin compañía." (p. 240) [loveless bed. (p. 249)]

Timón's motives in directing Félix's actions are by this point suspect. The reader's distrust of him is reinforced when he calls Félix's life "entertaining." As Timón's credibility as a trustworthy leader diminishes, his credibility as narrator disintegrates as well.

The narrator frequently refers to his direction of Félix as a script that he designs:

"Ojalá pudiese cotejar un día mi guión de probabilidades con la versión de las certezas de Félix. ¿En qué coincidiríamos? ¿En qué nos apartaríamos? ¿Cuál de las dos historias concluyentes sería la verdadera: la que yo me disponía a imaginar o la que él se disponía a vivir?"

(p. 239)

[Oh, if only one day I might compare my probable scenario with Felix's real version. Where would we coincide? Where would we differ? Which of the two endings would be the true one: the one I was preparing to invent, or the one he was preparing to live?]

(p. 248)

By its very nature, a script implies a guideline to which one must conform, a prompter of speech and action. Timón's use of this literary term to describe his relationship to Félix suggests his perception that the degree of control he exercises as a character extends to his role as a scriptwriter. Towards the end of the novel, Félix criticizes Timón for his "vocación de titiritero" (p. 241) [puppeteer's vocation], as he obviously feels trapped by the script imposed upon him by the narrator, who doubles as master spy.

As a scriptwriter, Timón sees himself as the one who determines Félix's activities from two vantage points: as the head of a spy organization and as narrator, with omnipotence that is relatively unchallenged in both capacities. Contrary to his assumptions, Félix is an individual struggling to keep his free will as a viable course of action. However, the narrator's perception is stubbornly arrested at the point where he sees Félix in his role as an agent and as a character in the script he has designed.

The issue is further problematized by the two endings to the novel—one proposed by the narrator, and the other one actually executed by Félix. It is Félix's version that dominates the narrative once he leaves the narrator's house, but the repetition of scenes at the end subverts Félix's appearance of control; thus, neither of their endings will be "la verdadera" [the true one].

After the retrieval of the hydra ring, Félix goes to Timón's house to rest for a week. At one point, Félix and Timón wrestle and Timón concedes that Félix is the victor. They then discuss future plans for Félix: he is to register to stay in the Geneva

Suites hotel and adopt the name of Diego Velázquez, as dictated by the Director General. Timón hopes thereby to remain informed of his enemy's plans.

The section ends with the narration's abrupt change to the future tense: "Fatalmente, regresará a las suites de la calle de Génova y pedirá la misma recámara que ocupó con anterioridad, el mismo lecho donde murió Sara Klein." (p. 240) [Inevitably, he will return to the suites de Génova and will ask for the same room, the room where Sara Klein died. (p. 249)] This use of the future tense represents Timón's attempt to reassert his control over Félix, again both as his boss (he tells him to assume the new identity) and as the scriptwriter. He wills that his script be followed through the appropriation of choices that are his as narrator. However, it is soon apparent that Félix has a plan of his own: he is determined to avenge Sara Klein's death. This plan carries out the plot of chivalric duty imposed on Félix, although he internalizes it to the extent that he believes it responds to a personal motivation. The plan causes Félix to pursue a different course of action than the one prescribed by the scriptwriter.

Timón, then, ultimately fails at his attempts to assert control, both over his spy operation and over the narration. These losses of control occur simultaneously, and serve to undermine both an individual and a traditional fictional construct. Presenting himself initially as an omnipotent scriptwriter and character, Timón's eventual demise leaves him as an impotent narrator, capable only of recording events, not of controlling them. Félix realizes that Timón is also Trevor, and as readers we acknowledge the narrator's direct involvement as a character in the events he orchestrates and narrates. When Timón refers to Chapters One through Thirty-Seven as his account of Félix's adventures, the result is a merging of scriptwriter and character, represented at the narrative level by the occasional insertion of a first-person perspective. Timón's failure as a character comes when he tries first to seduce Félix, then to dominate him, but fails on both counts and goes alone to his loveless bed.

When he gives Félix orders, Timón once again performs the role of a scriptwriter, and his use of the future tense attempts to ensure that his will be done. This constitutes the first ending. When Félix does otherwise—both on account of his vengeance of Sara's murder and due to the Director General's wishes—the second ending results. Félix's final assertion of his wishes over the scriptwriter's results in Timón's failure, as he loses authority and control over the narration's members.

Timón's status is uncertain in the end. The Director General now reasserts his control of the physical circumstances surrounding Félix: he moves him to the Hilton, assigns him a new name and a new job and, most significantly, interferes in what Félix believes is a most personal cause: the Director General shoots the presumed killer of Sara Klein that Félix had left to die in a meat locker. He again denies Félix a most basic freedom—to choose a course of action and then possess that act as one's own. This denial is compounded by the bitter irony that Félix's act is not his own, but the prescribed response to an internalized plot.

While he loses control over the events of the novel, Timón maintains an integral function within it, as narrator. This represents a reduction in power, since it strips him of any significant control. Having played the scriptwriter of the first two-thirds of the novel, Timón must acknowledge the Director General's reaffirmed control over his agent, Félix. Timón, too, eventually calls him Diego as if to acquiesce passively to the Director General's control. The narrator would like us to think that this is also part of his scriptwriter's plan to outwit his enemy. As Timón had stated earlier,

> "La partida se reiniciará. La próxima vez, sin embargo, se encontrarán con un adversario no sólo más fuerte, sino distinto. . . . No cometas el mismo error de nuestros enemigos. No me subestimes ni subestimes mis capacidades de metamorfosis."
>
> (p. 233)
>
> [The hand will be dealt again. The next time, however, they will run into an adversary that's not only stronger, but different. . . . Don't make the same mistake our enemies have made. Don't underestimate me nor my capabilities of metamorphosis.]

Timón would like to appear as if he were lying in wait, prepared at every turn to take on those forces more powerful than himself. However, the novel ends with the nearly exact repetition of two of the initial scenes, and the reader discovers that the narration is operating on its own circular momentum. Although the narrator might project a disguised control of the narrative, it is apparent that something or someone else is exercising even greater control, capable of orchestrating circularity.

In a scene that is nearly identical to the one at the beginning of the narrative, Félix finds himself in a "taxi colectivo" [collective taxi], with some of the same characters as before, and when he realizes that the initial scene is being repeated, he yells for the taxi to stop. When Félix arrives at the Presidential Palace for another awards ceremony, the uncanny resemblance of events is underscored by the stylistic slowing-down of the initial palace scene. Félix waits for the President to make his way down the line to greet him and, as he waits, he sees the same faces that he had seen before. The novel ends just as the President reaches Félix. With the exception of a name change, the final words of the novel are the same, as well: "El Señor Presidente estaba a unos cuantos metros de Diego Velázquez." (p. 282) [The President was within a few steps of Diego Velázquez. (p. 290)] Earlier in the novel, these words signal the initiation of Félix's adventures, whereupon he had plunged into a nightmarish whirlwind of events that would forever alter his existence.

The circularity of the ending of La cabeza de la hidra lends itself to various interpretations. It recalls the Indian past, steeped in fatalism and in a nonlinear perception of reality, and serves perhaps as a reminder to Félix that this is an undeniable component of his identity. Thus, in the next cycle he should incorporate the Indian factor, already part of his psyche, into his consciousness.

Gyurko's reading of the ending states that it is a positive one, arguing that Félix is transformed from an idealist living in a dream world into a "new, morally responsive" individual.[10] Thus, circularity might imply the possibility of a second chance for Félix to relive these events, but in a morally superior fashion.

However, an earlier conclusion in Gyurko's essay is far more likely:

> The protagonist is constantly forced back upon himself. The routes that he struggles to open up—the pathways towards self-actualization—are all consistently blocked. . . . Doubling is ultimately a fatalistic force that imprisons Félix within a series of mirrors of his own weak, vacillating, victimized self, until the protagonist finally is driven insane and totally accepts the role of Diego Velázquez.[11]

There is not enough left of Félix to accomplish such a morally demanding task. Even if one argues that to assume a new name is symbolic of a different consciousness of one's self, the fact remains that the original self has disintegrated, shredding the components of selfhood. In the postmodern world, these can no longer reconverge to become a reconstituted self. The notion of selfhood has been permanently altered, leaving no possibility for its return. Thus in a postmodern context the ending of La cabeza de la hidra is strongly negative.

Félix Maldonado assimilates the identity of Diego Velázquez because he feels absolutely powerless to impose his will any longer. This final loss of will comes as a result of Félix's discovery that his wife, Ruth, is the nun who stands as the murderer of Sara Klein. Back in his hotel room, Félix drifts into fitful delirium, murmuring the question, "Me doy, ¿quién gobierna al mundo, cómo voy a oponerme, no se puede con ellos, quiénes son, a quiénes obedecen ustedes, todos ustedes, me doy?" (p. 272) [I give up, who is it who rules the world? What can I do? I can't fight them, who are they? Why do you all obey? I give up. (p. 283)] This is labeled Félix Maldonado's last question; indeed, once he wakes up, he is referred to only as Diego Velázquez. The imagery of resurrection is clear: in the death of sleep, Félix leaves the old man behind and awakes to become the new. Félix will now function exclusively as the Licenciado Diego Velázquez.

The adoption of a new identity is no guarantee that he will respond differently to the same series of events, in an opportunity to assert himself with a newly defined sense of identity. Rather, the nearly exact repetition of scenes is profoundly pessimistic, as all signs point to an eventual and equally frustrated demise of the self, whether the individual is named Félix or Diego. The cycle is fated since Diego, too, is destined to be a victim of external forces far more powerful than himself.

As noted earlier, the character who doubles as both scriptwriter and narrator experiences the same fate. Having failed to impose his control over Félix both as his captain, Timón, and as selector of narrative events, the narrator also is excluded from regaining control in the future, since the narrative is circular. There is a force external to his control and to his knowledge that manipulates the narrative elements, regardless of Timón's own script. Even the Director General's satisfaction at Félix's acceptance of the identity of Diego Velázquez, with all its implicit acknowledgment of control, is superseded by the circularity of the narration. In the novel, circularity is not attributed to any source; it is instead a systemic agent. The eventual domination of circularity, however, speaks for its supremacy and leads the reader to the conclusion that the text operates under a wider sphere of knowledge and control.

Postmodernity subscribes to the notion of widening circles of awareness that are in conflict with each other. It thereby repudiates the possibility of a final, all-inclusive circle and favors instead a paradigm of overlapping circular configurations. This notion is present throughout *La cabeza de la hidra*. After Félix relates to Timón his version of the events of the past two weeks, Timón states that it is now necessary for him to provide the larger perspective of events: "Ahora me correspondía a mí darle la versión de los hechos, la versión global de lo que Félix sólo había vivido y comprendido parcialmente." (p. 219) [Now I will give my own interpretation, the broad perspective that Felix lived but only partially understood. (p. 228)]

The narrator makes clear the implication that he has access to privileged information, as if he possesses the broad perspective common to narrators. However, as we have shown, the circular structure of the novel subverts this notion as it wrests control from the narrator of *La cabeza de la hidra*. In a moment reminiscent of Borges, the dreamer who has dreamed a man suddenly realizes that he, too, is within someone else's dream (or script).

In this manner, Fuentes subverts the traditional representation of the narrator. He bases his presentation on the postmodern tenet that final authority rests with no one, since complete knowledge of all truth is the prerequisite for such authority. The anti-absolutist view to which postmodernism subscribes makes it impossible to ascertain definitive truth, since many truths exist, both within and without our limited spheres of awareness. Complete knowledge is therefore unattainable.

Fuentes's selection of genre facilitates the narrative expression of this postmodern theme of the novel. The detective genre constructs its narrative on the principle of the delayed disclosure of fact. As clues are found, characters' spheres of knowledge are extended and overlap with each other, and new evidence changes previous conclusions. Definitive conclusions cannot be made until all the facts are known, and the sleuth spends the course of the novel in pursuit of conclusive evidence. The narration is only loosely chronological; the appearance of new information interrupts the linear sequence as characters will digress and reconsider in search of some breakthrough clue. Thus, the action moves in erratic patterns, shifting backwards as often as it does forward, guided by the search for additional knowledge.

A number of postmodern suppositions are inherent in the structure of the detective genre. Different characters' awareness of facts follows a hierarchical order. In the postmodernist view, no single individual reaches the uppermost tier; instead, people's knowledge is considered on a comparative scale. Since new information is constantly being introduced, conclusions are always shifting and are never definitive. The process of arriving at hypothetical conclusions is the more significant activity. Additionally, the nonsequential discovery of fact underscores postmodernism's minimalization of causality.

Carlos Fuentes also makes use of the detective genre by subverting its conventions in order to introduce alternative postmodern presentations of the assumptions behind the genre's forms. *La cabeza de la hidra* is told retrospectively, and it is implied that the narrator knows the final outcome. The circularity of the narration, however, simultaneously defers the finality of a resolution and discredits the scriptwriter's omniscience and his omnipotence. Thus, the narrative succumbs to the circular fate of the narrator and of the protagonist.

Finally, in his break with the modernist segregation of high and low art, Fuentes creates a text that is a mixture of both forms. It is rich in texture, utilizing the popular form of the detective novel, but injecting it with sophisticated subversions relative to postmodernity. McNerney and Martin, among others, have commented on the cinematic intertextuality that provides a frame of reference for many characters in the novel. Many of the films mentioned are also plebian in nature, reflecting the patrimony of the masses ("Casablanca" and "The Maltese Falcon," for instance). Others include specialized references with which fewer moviegoers would be familiar—for instance, Japanese films or lesser-known films from the thirties.

The presence of paintings in this novel, both classical and modern, has been extensively studied by Lanin Gyurko and Mary E. Davis. Samples of art representing high culture range from Velázquez to Ricardo Martínez, a contemporary Mexican artist. The incorporation of visual art ranges from graphic depiction of the state of the novel's characters in Martínez's paintings[12] to the ultimate expression of intertextuality, when Velázquez becomes the double of Fuentes.[13]

Literary models latent in the pages of *La cabeza de la hidra* have also been documented by Davis. Sources range from writers of detective fiction, such as Dashiel Hammett, to Poe; of particular interest is Fuentes's use of excerpts from Shakespeare and Lewis Carroll. As the basis for Timón's secret code, these epigraphs represent the juxtaposition of high and low art consistent throughout the narration.

In conclusion, a careful reading of *La cabeza de la hidra* reveals the novel's postmodern concerns. Both the utilization and the subversion of the conventions of the detective genre provide structural and thematic vehicles for the exploration of postmodern thought. The detective's step-by-step gathering of the facts of a case illustrate the hierarchies of awareness by which the world operates. Postmodernism questions the claim of full knowledge of all data, and deems it imperative that we realize that this process of gradually assimilating new spheres of awareness is never complete. Timón's subjective rendering of events calls readers to reconsider the entirety of what has been placed before them, underscoring the fact that this scriptwriter's is one of many versions of the story. Although the protagonist of *La cabeza de la hidra* eventually solves the case, and although the scriptwriter controls much of the narration, the fact that neither of them masters their significant projects suggests a broader scenario, one that they cannot see, and in the end they must both acknowledge their limitation.

As the postmodern tenet of stages of awareness is applied to the narrative, the view of fiction as continual process is formally underscored by the novel's circular structure. Timón's inability to control the outcome of events, as well as Félix's participation in determining that outcome, contribute to the novel's own susceptibility to outside forces.

Always hesitant to credit the narrator with any definitive authority, the novel is crafted to undermine with subtlety. Timón's traditional role of autonomy and determining control is rejected, and Fuentes paints instead a picture of a broken, misguided individual. In this novel, the narrator is a pitiful creature, whose shrill appropriation of authority is made all the worse by his refusal to acknowledge his less-than-omniscient status in the text.

As the novel comes full circle and moves beyond our own sphere of awareness, we turn our attention, along with Fuentes, to the role of the reader in the construction of a story, or in the creation of a literary text. In *Cristóbal Nonato*, the radical expectations placed upon the reader, as well as on other aspects of the narrative, place great strain on the traditional text. In its experimentation with generic form, *La cabeza de la hidra* is a clear precursor to this most linguistically experimental novel to date. The following chapter discusses this new and engaging expression of postmodern fiction, as Fuentes gives literary form to his preoccupation with issues of readership, collective identity, and the textual process itself.

4

Issues of National and Narrative Control: *Cristóbal Nonato* (1987)

CRISTÓBAL NONATO (1987) ISSUES A PROPHETIC DECLARATION OF Mexico's fate in 1992, the five-hundredth anniversary of the Old World's encounter with the New. The commemoration of such a significant historical event lends itself to meditation on the process of the formation of a Mexican identity, and in the novel Fuentes examines the frustrated, corrupted state of political and social affairs in modern Mexico. Fuentes's customary linguistic and formal experimentation here serve to underscore the thematic intent of subversion of scripted, conventional systems and institutions. Issues of control, then, are central to the novel.

Critics and reviewers have noted in the novel a return to the thematic and formal emphases of Fuentes's early works, namely *La región más transparente* (1958) and *La muerte de Artemio Cruz* (1962). Along with *La cabeza de la hidra* (1978), *Cristóbal Nonato* completes the triptych initiated at the outset of his novelistic trajectory. The depiction of Mexico City in these three novels represents the destiny of a fractured, forgetful nation, and explores through narrative and linguistic experimentation the limits of the text. In *Cristóbal Nonato*, the treatment of thematic and formal concerns can best be understood within the context of postmodernity, which assumes a fundamental relativity that necessitates a fiction open to variance. The novel's nontraditional aspects are thus grounded in postmodern perspectives.

Mexico in 1992 is a nation in disarray to the extent that Cristóbal's mother asks three unanswered questions: What language will he speak? What air will he breathe? What will his name be? Fuentes addresses issues of contemporary Mexico that recur throughout his novelistic production: the preservation of a cultural identity, represented by a national language and territory; environmental concerns (namely pollution and consumerism) that symbolize the rights and responsibilities of citizenry; and the recognition of the need for a defined sense of self, that is inscribed in the naming of individuals.

In *Cristóbal Nonato*, Fuentes amplifies the fate of Félix Maldonado in *Cabeza de la hidra*, gauging the probable effects of similar causalties to the identity of a nation. Felix's susceptibility to external influences finds its broader parallel in Mexico's vulnerability to foreign powers. As Félix's appearance was altered, so now the nation's territory has been decimated: U.S. oil companies have appropriated the northern states of Mexico and have renamed it Mexamerica, housing eighty million Hispanics expelled from the United States. The northern oil fields have been seized to pay Mexico's foreign debt, but oil production has been controlled so that only the interest is paid, thus guaranteeing the long-term foreign control of Mexican oil. Mexamerica is neither nurtured nor protected by its isolation from the outside world: guerrillas threaten the internal stability of the region, and those Mexicans wishing to preserve their cultural identity flee to the South. Fuentes offers a postmodern illustration in demonstrating the devastation of the large-scale imposition of conformity.

It is appropriate therefore to consider the significance of the novel's title. Cristóbal is named in honor of Christopher Columbus, and the novel discusses the origin of this name: "igual en todas las lenguas . . . Portador de Cristo y Paloma o sea las dos personas que faltan de la Trinidad, el Hijo y el Espíritu Santo, nuestro Descubridor." [The same in all languages . . . Christbearer and Dove, which is to say, the two persons missing from the Trinity, the Son and the Holy Spirit, our Discoverer.][1] The satirical tone is obvious, mocking the joint venture of Spanish religious and military domination. Of particular importance in light of the five-hundredth anniversary of the "discovery" of America that it evokes, *Cristóbal Nonato* stands against the hegemony of colonial domination. The title also recalls the Latin phrase announcing the birth of Christ ("Cristus natus est"); its denial of the birth of a savior anticipates the apocalyptic tone of the novel.

The ecological plight of Mexico, particularly as a result of the petroleum industry, is of related importance. The repeated references to smog and contaminated rain as "la mierda llovida del cielo," (p. 29) [the shit that rained down from heaven. (p. 21)] make clear the negative effects of the abuse of this natural resource that has been problematic for Mexico since the beginning of its oil industry. The government's promotion of consumerism comes in the forms of slogans that encourage wastefulness:

"MEXICO TIENE ENERGIA PARA BOTAR." (p. 53) [MEXICO
HAS ENERGY TO BURN. (p. 44)]

Scatological imagery abounds in the novel, announcing Mexico's fate of being buried by the "shit in the air." As Cristóbal is
being conceived on the beaches of Acapulco, his parents, Angel
and Angeles, are defecated upon by a diarrhea-stricken Homero
as he parachutes. In a kind of baptism of excrement, Cristóbal,
and thus his entire generation, is doomed to a future burdened
with the environmental crisis.

In Cristóbal Nonato, then, Fuentes reexamines the ecological
concerns present in his first publication, a collection of short
stories (Los días enmascarados, 1954). In "El que inventó la
pólvora" [The Gunpowder Inventor], consumerism is rampant,
due to the effects of nuclear weaponry that cause the disintegration of all materials within a matter of minutes. The streets of
Mexico City are covered by mountains of trash. Consistent in
tone with the 1987 novel, this story's apocalyptic vision shows
the alteration of Mexico's territory: the narrator swims at a beach
that wasn't there before. In the novel, Cristóbal recalls an earlier
time when children could swim in prepolluted waters.

The lure of the North is depicted in ridiculous proportions in
the novel. Jipi Toltec, named for the Aztec god and currently a
member of the Four Jodiditos rock group, routinely brings his
mother electric appliances and gadgets from the United States,
even though she does not have electricity in her shanty. The
unquestioning assimilation of U.S. culture and commodities, regardless of their practicality or benefit to the Mexican consumer,
is a frequent target of Fuentes's satire.

As in La región más transparente, no single character occupies
the role of protagonist; rather, the novel portrays Mexican society
through a collage of figures, who represent different societal aspects. Thematic unity is provided by the nontraditional narrator,
a fetus, Cristóbal, who throughout the nine chapters of his physical and literary gestation describes the view from the womb. This
unlikely narrative premise inaugurates the novel's ludic relationship to language and to the conventions of the novelistic form,
making Cristóbal Nonato a literary playground for both author
and reader.

The narrator is reduced to a nonentity, a marginalized member
of society with uncertain rights and privileges. Fuentes's sugges-
tive presentation of a fetus that can in fact reason, equipped with
the knowledge of generations that is transmitted to him through
his genes, also lends Cristóbal the freedom to shape himself in

his narrative role. His omniscient status indicates that he exists in a hyperspace: he is within his mother's womb, and thus he does not interact with the external world that he hears and sees. He is incapable of transmitting any message beyond the boundaries of the womb, except to the reader. This breaks open the traditional presentation of the novel, as the narrator taps into the reader's experience in a silent but communicative act that extends beyond the womb and the pages of the text. The pattern in Cristóbal Nonato of continual movement from the individual to the collective takes place, then, at this very basic level. Reaching into the minds of individual readers, Cristóbal voices his concerns for the world into which he is about to be born, and demands the reader's participation in determining his fate.

Other characters represent different segments of contemporary Mexican society, often positioned in an oppositional stance to each other. The result is a varied portraiture of extremes, each figure reduced to a simplification of a worldview. Angel Palomar, Cristóbal's father, is the son of wealthy scientists with a social conscience who die while attempting to solve the problem of world hunger with a "Taco Inconsumible." He is orphaned at an early age, but he remembers a photograph of Heisenberg, the German physicist who proposed the theory of simultaneous realities. Angel spends much of the novel trying to recover a balance to his ideological and sexual convictions, and concludes that he is a rebellious conservative. He holds several beliefs simultaneously, and although he never resolves the disparities in his ideology, he manages to achieve a relative state of ideological synthesis.

In contrast to the idealistic father of her child, Angeles (the names might indicate ideological counterparts) is consistently the practical one, asking severely realistic questions about the world into which her son would be born. Her queries range widely into linguistic concerns; she wonders what one should say when words are not enough. Angeles seems to have no past, but this results in a rare awareness of her consequent vulnerability to every passing fashion, from environmentalism to twenties-style clothing. She refuses to position herself as a victim when Angel leaves her during her pregnancy. In her resolution to look forward to raising a child alone, Angeles exhibits an uncommon independence from her male companion.

The oppositional strategies of presentation of these figures underscore a central thematic concern of the novel. When Angel returns to Angeles on the eve of her delivery, they have each abandoned the polarities of their previous positions, meeting somewhere in the middle. Angel has concluded that the love between two individuals is revolution enough, and returns to dedicate himself to loving Angeles. She has learned to combine practicality and fantasy, thus fulfilling Angel's perceived needs. Their subsequent decision to remain in Mexico and raise their child there is a direct result of their new position between extremes, finding a suitable space in the gaps left by polarities.

Angel's uncle, Fernando Benítez, is a figure modeled after the contemporary Mexican historian and student of Indian culture. In the novel, Fernando represents good-hearted advocacy on behalf of the Indian, speaking their language and respectfully sitting at their side to learn from them. Homero Fagoaga, Angel's other uncle and Fernando's nemesis, is a pompous, obese bigot who disinherits Angel in an attempt to force him to change his ideological position. Fernando and Homero embody opposite worldviews and as in most other cases described in *Cristóbal Nonato*, their differences are never resolved. Instead, they warily observe each other, often engaging in word battles. In the process of their reactive opposition, countless misunderstandings and abuses occur, and the distance between the two is never reduced.

The corruption of its leaders is a significant reason for the current conditions in Mexico. Ulises López, government "Superminister," manipulates economic power structures for his own gain, betraying Mexico in the process. Ulises's life is structured around the pursuit of wealth and his wife, Lucha, is a caricature of materialism. She considers her first shopping trip to Houston a transcendent event of mystical proportions, and desires that Mexico be annexed to the United States so that she won't have to leave the country to do her shopping.

The López's have made themselves wealthy from the nation's poverty. Lucha has caused many innocent deaths by setting fire to the squatters' shacks gathered on the periphery of her property. Ultimately, Ulises's philosophy involves a rigid hypocrisy of word and action. He provides guidelines for what to say in public and in private: "En público:—La producción somos todos. En privado:—Este país se divide en productores y parásitos." (p. 365) [In public: "We are all involved in production." In private: "This country is divided into producers and parasites." (p. 339)] His conception of speech as two separate discourses not only suggests that he is internally warring with his conscience, but it also leaves an unresolved polarization. In Ulises, Fuentes presents another character whose awareness of a divided self prevents him from synthesis into a whole figure. Ulises's life ends violently, at the hands of angry squatters, reenacting a historically scripted fate of the abusive rich.

Following a general pattern of the novel, the toll of opportunistic attitudes of individuals has its collective counterpart. The creation of Mexamerica is a direct result of the corruption and selfishness of those engaged in opportunistic dealings with foreign investors. Combined with a national overdependence on oil, the motion comes full circle as individuals again become victims of collective action.

In the case of Acapulco, Fuentes portrays the potential effects of a wholesale acculturation to the American way of life. Separated from Central Mexico by a Taco Curtain, this traditional haven for North-American tourists is an extreme expression of cultural betrayal. Originally an escapist resort area, Acapulco is now an insulated territory, its borders carefully monitored. New York strip steak and U.S. toilet paper are among the items brought into the region by the likes of Bubble Gómez, an albino who has rejected his roots to the point of bleaching his Spanish and Indian blood. Apocapulco, as it is termed, meets the fate of inevitable destruction, a consequence of its impoverished sense of Mexican identity.

The Mexican Revolution lurks in the background of the events of the novel, functioning as a constant reminder of the betrayal of subsequent generations to its cause. During the eighty years since the Revolution, individuals have abandoned the aims of equality and of nationhood. The only individual who still believes in these revolutionary ideals is Cristóbal's great-grandfather, General Rigoberto Palomar, who suffers from revolutionary dementia: "Un hombre cuerdo en todo lo demás . . . convenciéndose de dos cosas simultánea y contradictoriamente: 1) la Revolución no había terminado y 2) la Revolución había triunfado y cumplido todas sus promesas." (p. 77) [[A man] . . . who was sane on all other matters. . . . He simultaneously held two contradictory beliefs: (1) The Revolution was not over; and (2) the Revolution had triumphed and carried out all its promises. (p. 67)] Obviously, not all promises have been met, but nonetheless the Revolution did end. Things are not as black and white as they once were, but General Palomar's inability to accept this causes him to leave the conclusions permanently unresolved. His instability is symptomatic of his generation's inability to reconcile reality with the rhetoric expressed through the government, which continues its revolutionary hype without promoting or executing permanent action. Federico Robles Chacón is a powerful politician whose manipulation of mass mentality is a *tour de force*, which calls attention to the presentation of media in the text. He is the son of the *Región* character, who betrays the ideals of the Revolution and assimilates false (foreign) values. In *Cristóbal Nonato*, Federico Robles Chacón, as a representative member of the second post-Revolution generation, offers little promise of aiding the failing status of Mexican unity. The solution he proposes as a member of the government are brilliant but superfluous to socioeconomic realities: he fashions the image of Mamadoc (perhaps the potentially vicious Mexican counterpart of Papa Doc, the Haitian dictator) as a cultural sign, someone to whom the average Mexican can look as a symbol of national identity. He predicts that the masses will fervently pledge their loyalty to her as the embodiment of their Mexican selves, thus staving off revolt by effectively turning their attention away from the incompetent Mexican president, whose economic reforms are nonexistent.

Mamadoc is a mixture of Mae West, the Virgin of Guadalupe, Malinche, Adelita, Coatlicue, and "doña Bárbara en helicóptero." (p. 40) ["Doña Bárbara in a helicopter. (p. 32)] Federico Robles Chacón selects a very ordinary, patriotic secretary (she wears hair ribbons in the colors of the Mexican flag), and from her impoverished being creates a powerful persona whom the masses soon cheer as their venerated Mamadoc. The politician's creation embodies a wide selection of national symbols where there is something for everyone: Mamadoc is Adelita, the barefoot, humble Mexican peasant; Mae West, the unattainable Anglo movie star about whom Mexican men fantasize; she is also the Virgin of Guadalupe and Malinche, thus the dual saint/whore image is incarnated, the double standard bred by the trademark Mexican *machismo*. Mamadoc is also Coatlicue, a reminder of the Indian past, but in purely superficial form: no longer the powerful mother of the gods in a skirt of serpents, Coatlicue becomes a cultural token of ephemeral value. Once again, the past is either denied or forgotten, and the consequences are potentially irremediable.

The creation of Mamadoc, an embodiment of collective perceptions of Mexican identity, occurs before our very eyes. Robles's manipulation of cultural elements reveals the scripted nature of this construct. It likewise calls into question the media-produced image of mass culture, subverting its practice of legitimization as the text reveals the crafted nature of such expressions of collective identity. Fuentes's conclusion is that the particular signs of Mexican culture are not an inherent part of the national entity; they are often the product of skillful manipulation by those in power.

As the vehicle of institutionalized expression, the media promote the discourses of power. This is particularly true in the case of the government, as it is positioned in opposition to the people of Mexico. Fuentes depicts the corruption of motives and the means of its ministers, but he also narrows his eyes at the institutions' use of technology and media to ensure that their programs are executed to their satisfaction. The hype of slogans is a common expression of the discourse of power, yet Fuentes's obvious mockery of this means of promotion results in a shrill falsetto that undercuts all respect for what is being promoted.

The deliberately farcical presentation of the government occurs throughout the novel. Fuentes's severest criticism is directed toward the government's abuse of power, as he holds its agents accountable for the extent of their influence. The minister, Ulises López, and Homero Fagoaga have created an internal system of corruption in which they profit from selling pesticides banned in the United States to the Philippines. Homero's flippant response is symbolic of the government's: "Es preferible tener inversiones y empleo, aunque sea con cáncer y enfisema!" (p. 98). [It's better to have investments and a job, even if they bring cancer and emphesyma! (p. 89)][2]

Implicit in the slogan-like presentation of the governmental decrees is cynicism toward the media, as well. The government-sponsored contest that results in Cristóbal's conception is an example. In honor of the historical significance of 1992, the first son to be born at 0:00 hours on 12 October 1991 and bearing the name Cristóbal, will be proclaimed leader of the Mexican nation. Mamadoc makes the announcement, and numerous slogans are posted: "MACHO MEXICANO, EMBARAZA A TU SEÑORA, PERO YA!" (p. 14) [MEXICAN MACHOS, IMPREGNATE YOUR WIVES—RIGHT AWAY! (p. 6)]

The publicity for the contest for a national Regent is studded with contradictions, ridiculously illogical and obviously appealing to collective sentiment: "¡A procrear, pues, señoras y señores! ¡Su placer es su deber y su deber es su libertad! ¡En México todos somos libres y el que no quiera ser libre será castigado! ¡Y confíen ustedes en sus jueces! Alguna vez les hemos fallado?" (p. 14) [So, ladies and gentlemen, let's get procreating! Your pleasure is your duty and your duty is your freedom! In Mexico we are all free and anyone who does not want to be free should be punished! You can count on your judges, after all: have we ever let you down? (p. 6)] The systems of mass communication are simply an extension of bureaucracy; the same theories of mass manipulation apply.

Central to these theories is the issue of control. Institutions package their ideology in trite codes of meaning in order to regulate the projection of selected images. These codes are necessarily flexible, easily manipulated in order to dominate more successfully. As Ulises López states: "La información es el poder. La no información es más poder." (p. 288) [Information is Power. No Information Is More Power. (p. 262)] The positioning of those who hold information becomes the determinant for the measure of control they exhibit; as transmitters, representatives of institutions are able to withold information, to control the message.

Nationalized television as an instrument of mass manipulation provides such an illustration in the novel. Subliminal messages are inserted in split-second spots. Mamadoc's slogan, "UNION Y OLVIDO" [UNION AND OBLIVION], flashes in the midst of daily programming twenty-four hours a day. Fuentes's satirical exaggeration of governmental propaganda comes in the form of its reduction to one insistent, vacant phrase.

Even stronger is Fuentes's attack on the government's presentation of falsehood as truth: the arrest of a policeman accepting the bribe of an American tourist, the turning over of golf courses to the poor, retroactive justice applied to the fat cats of past regimes. Staged to appear real, television serves government strategy to create a false image, to hide their political agenda. "Todo es falso, todo es preparado, nada de lo que ustedes ven está ocurriendo realmente, pero todo es presentado como un hecho que las cámaras acaban de sorprender." (p. 313) [Every single event is false, it's all made up, nothing of what you're seeing is really happening, but it's all presented as a fact freshly caught by the camera. (p. 286)] Fuentes thus textually illustrates the constructed nature of ideology, in portraying all messages the government sends as propaganda.

The subliminal arm-twisting of the media is further illustrated by another character in the novel, the Ayatollah Matamoros who, according to Maarten van Delden, "eventually mesmerizes the masses with an ideological mishmash composed of Mexican machismo, religious fundamentalism and 60s liberationism—all delivered with the most up-to-date communication techniques."[3] It is significant that the Ayatollah is a frustrated writer, and that in order to vent his anguish at his lack of verbal expression he resorts to violence. He adopts the voice of high-tech mass media, and thereby appropriates a discourse of power that is violent in its hold over people. For Carlos Fuentes, the discourse of media is clearly suspect.

Also of note in *Cristóbal Nonato* is the presentation of governmental rhetoric and cultural shortcutting. Reyes-Tatinclaux analyzes Fuentes' subversion of official discourse, and attributes its subversion to a desire to refute the thought patterns latent in a corrupt government's language.[4] This critic correctly points to the use of ideological antagonism, the demythification of democracy, and an extreme use of slogans. (p. 102) Furthermore, *Cristóbal Nonato* unmasks the free-market ideology and trademark American individualism that the United States proclaims in its dealings with Mexico. But the novel presents these constructs as agents of imperialism and a convenient cover for the U.S.'s self-promoting disregard of any other country. In the name of peacekeeping, for instance, President Dumble Danger (a.k.a. Trigger Trader, Rumboldt Ranger, Wrinkle Wrecker, obvious references to Ronald Reagan), sends twenty thousand U.S. Marines to occupy Veracruz. They are determined not to create the image of another Vietnam: their shacks are designed to last only six months, and soldiers are rotated every 179 days, so that no one is there longer than the term allowed by international regulations. But the oppression of the jungle and the use of chemical warfare overshadow artificial attempts to present this invasion differently.

The "Priest of Death," Reverend Royall Payne, is a veteran of the U.S. occupation of several Central American countries in the eighties and promotes a fundamentalist brand of religious fanaticism. In an outrageous coupling of military might and spiritual fervor, he televises a weekly religious broadcast from his Apache helicopter in Veracruz, dressed in a black jacket with ammunition rounds strapped across his chest, and says the Lord has told him, "Sal y sé mi soldado extermina a mis enemigos y entonces te recibiré y tendrás el placer que soy Yo!" (p. 521) [Go forth and be my soldier exterminate my enemies and then I shall receive you and you will have the pleasure which I am! (p. 491)] It is a scenario closely resembling the colonial domination of Spanish forces five hundred years earlier, when loyalty to God and crown, and an individualist fortune-seeking mentality motivated the soldiers. In the novel, Fuentes depicts the deformation of individual patriotism and loyalty to country when it is codified and imposed as a defense of national military and economic interests. He exposes the hidden agendas of the institution of army and government, discrediting its discourse and the religious one that supports it, by an outlandish exaggeration of its means of promotion.

At the same time, the novel strives not to replace the official discourse of institutions with an equally rigid substitute. Instead, Fuentes looks to language itself as source of creations that are continually new, composing much of *Cristóbal Nonato* from linguistic experimentation that breaks new ground in the conception of the text. This is accomplished at both the individual and corporate level in a productive positioning of the linguistic system as both personalized and nationalized discourse.

Cristóbal Nonato manifests a postmodern stance toward the text as a fictional construct, based primarily on its view of language. Cristóbal summarizes the essence of the novel's view of language when he speaks of his own language that develops, as he does, within the womb:

> "Mi lenguaje y sus símbolos se desarrollan muchísimo antes de que yo tenga que hacer uso práctico de la lengua para comunicarme; mi actual vida intrauterina ya es parte de ese largo desarrollo del lenguaje y sus signos. . . . Yo voy a comunicarme independientemente del vocabulario, la sintaxis y los símbolos del mundo que me espera al nacer."
>
> (p. 105)
>
> [My language and its symbols develop much earlier than when I have to make practical use of language to communicate; my current intrauterine life is already part of that long process of development of language and its signs. . . . I am going to communicate independently of the vocabulary, the syntax and the symbols of the world that awaits me upon my birth.]

The result is a language, and therefore a text, intent on following its creative discursive impulses.

Language in the novel sustains a creative, not a mimetic, relationship to reality. The arbitrary nature of linguistic signs is exemplified through associative linguistic games, puns, and the predilection of sound in passages that are akin to the improvisations of a jazz musician. As in poetry, the sounds of words play an integral part in fashioning the text. Alliteration lends an associative logic to passages, as the meandering of sounds often takes the narrative on a rhythm of its own. The early poetry of Octavio Paz is recalled in Fuentes's description of Cristóbal's conception as Angel approaches Angeles, slithering up to her on the beach: "Culebra, ceba, culea, celebra, cerebra."[5] There is a relatively easy metonymic transition between these words until the fifth one, which on the auditory level belongs to this list, but which conceptually pushes the reader to·a different set of associations.

Puns run rampant through the pages of the novel, many of them crossing over into other languages; for instance, "Qué disco escuchamos (el último del millón de discos: el Immanuel Can't), mejor kántame algo tú." (p. 117) [What record should I put on (the last one put out by my favorite group, Immanuel Can't), well, Kan't you sing me something? (p. 99)] As Julio Ortega states, "The pun unties language from its function and turns it into a lavish spectacle, a flexible material, plastic, capable of remolding its representations, but capable at the same time of fostering criticism, irony, humor."[6] Word play through changes in spelling are frequent as well: Juana Lógica, Isabel la Caótica, Tour Quemada, Inky Sesión, Robas Pié. (p. 555) [Queen Juana the Madder of Fact, Isabel the Chaotic, tour brulee, Inky Session, Rubberspyre. (p. 523)] The result is usually humorous, and always laced with satire.

The welcome interference of other languages permeates the narrative, creating an inventive cross-reference in word play. Neologisms abound, for example, "lentes johnlenones" (p. 11) [John Lennonish (p. 3)] and "cromohidrosis." (p. 14) [cromohydrosis. (p. 7)] The phonetic transcription of English into Spanish also allows for new semantic combinations: "No te me friquées" (p. 121) and "Ol tugueder náu" (p. 166).[7] Tomasito, Homero's Philippino servant, filters what he hears through Tagalog, lending hilarity to Homero's excitable insistence on the correctness of language.

Typographic form in the novel also expresses its freedom. Borrowing from concrete poetry, the novel expresses visually the semantic value of a phrase: "Las palabras se le fueron muriendo en la boca" (p. 36) begins on one line and ends seven or eight lines down [his words died right in his mouth (p. 27)]; the words trail off the page, mimicking the speaker's voice. Slogans and printed ads written in upper case smatter the text like graffiti.

In its utilization of language, Cristóbal Nonato rejects prescribed relationships between signifier and signified, and thereby subscribes to a poststructuralist view of language. There is no inherent meaning to language; its signs are arbitrary and flexible, and become temporary receptacles of meaning because of relationships that are imposed upon them.

The text of *Cristóbal Nonato* is littered with individualized linguistic expression. Fuentes challenges the notion of an absolute language system, inscribing instead the unorthodox, or utilizing a particular discourse around which to construct a figure, thereby underscoring its artificiality as a codified expression. Cristóbal makes up his own version of language as he develops physically, growing with language. The atemporality and omniscience of the womb provide him with an ideal environment in which to express himself, unhindered by the structures of time and by a solely first-person discourse.

The personalized discourse of Ada Ching could be said to be "intocada por los oráculos de la sybilización" (p. 181) [untouched by the oracles of sybilization (p. 164)], creating her own reduced orbit of language. Her character recalls those of Severo Sarduy in its racial mixture of French, Chinese—and here—Mexican. This cultural background forces her language to be hybrid, a heterogenous activity of internalized associations between word and meaning that are continually shifting:

> "Estoy buleversada, los invito a bufear la noche del revellón, todo sobre cuenta propia para excusarnos de la blaga del garzón, no era malo, sólo jugetón vendrían todos de vuelta al disco, prometido y jurado? los minetes de la banda que tocaban tan ravisantes iban a tocar más bonitamente que jamás y ahora todos a debrullarse solos!"[8]

Utilizing a system of linguistic association that is mostly unintelligible, Ada Ching's linguistic expression follows its own particular logic, a system closed to all but Ada herself. Again, the result points to the insufficiency of language as receptacle of independent or absolute meaning based on an inherent association between signifier and signified. What is left in language, and what becomes the catalyst for communication, is an intuitive interpretation of sounds.

Angel's aunts, Capitolina and Farnesia, employ a paratactic discourse, positioning rejoinders in nonsensical combinations. While at dinner, they disturb the guests with their inconsequential and nonsequitur chatter:

> '—Hacen cajeta en Celaya y panochitas en Puebla. Niégueme usted eso! Atrévase!
> El asombro de los huéspedes no era consolado por Farnesia, quien alternaba la conversación de su hermana con inconsecuencias verbales de todo género:
> —No importa. Jamás aceptaremos una invitación suya . . .

—Ya que hablas de tacos, sentenciaba Capitolina, no puedo hablar de tacos sin pensar en tortillas . . .
—Entre paréntesis, comentaba Farnesia, y en tercer lugar, nosotras nunca . . .'

(p. 81)

["They make jam in Celaya and sugar candy in Puebla. Are you going to deny it! I dare you!"
The shock of the guests was not assuaged by Farnesia, who interrupted her sister's conversation with verbal inconsequentialities of all sorts:
"It doesn't matter. We shall never accept an invitation from you . . ."
"Now that you mention tacos," Capitolina pronounced, "I can't talk about tacos without thinking of tortillas."
"Incidentally," Farnesia commented, "and in the third place, we never . . ."]

(p. 71)

Although they employ clichés and trite expressions, the ordering patterns the aunts utilize render them unintelligible. The loss of a proper context drains their language of meaning; were they to be freed from clichés, and acknowledge the relativistic fluidity of words, their odd syntax might engender meaning. However, Capitolina and Farnesia's political ideology is reflected in their language. They are members of the Mexican aristocracy, and their linguistic expression is as stilted as their political and social perspectives (radical conservativism and fundamental Catholicism), and as fossilized as their ancient furniture. Their discourse could only be revolutionized by a reevaluation of the past that they prefer remain unchanged.

The figure of the Chilean actress and *bolero* singer, Concha Toro, utilizes the language of the *bolero* as her reference point, and she customarily speaks with lines from a song. Her entire being revolves around musical expression, an appropriate combination of sound and meaning. Concha adopts the culturally grounded discourse of the *bolero* as a foreigner in Mexico, thus twice removing her own linguistic expression from a collective, certified language.

In contrast, Homero is a linguist and member of the Academia de la Lengua. Adopting a most traditional, almost seventeenth-century Spanish syntax, Homero sees himself as the Cid Lenguador, savior of the Spanish language. He expresses himself in the most pompous of euphuistic phrases, as when he excuses a woman's flatulence:

'No ofendo con las que me siento, señora marquesa, si le digo que la siguiente flatulencia de su merced corre por mi cuenta; usted siga nomás comiendo este platillo excelso de la cocina nacional, los frijoles refritos con sus rajas y su queso manchego y sus chicharrones, no faltaba más.'

(p. 70)

["I do not offend through those with which I sit down, Marquise, if I say that your ladyship's next flatulence will figure on my bill; you just go on eating this sublime dish from our national cuisine, refried beans, slices of onion, Manchego cheese, and peas, who could want more?"]

(p. 61)

Homero embodies the formal rigidity of Academy-certified discourse, which is also suspect because it implies standardization, a neutralizing of linguistic difference. Fuentes utilizes this character as a parody of institutionalized expression, such as the discourse of academicians.

At the collective level, Fuentes's portrayal of language in *Cristóbal Nonato* communicates the thematic concerns of the novel. The cultural identity of Mexico is threatened by the decomposition of its language. As mentioned previously, the lack of Spanish punctuation is consistent throughout the novel. Fuentes demonstrates the ease with which such a significant change could occur in the future, highlighting the vulnerability of such time-honored and now culturally integral traditions. This is reminiscent of the recent motion by a faction within the Spanish Royal Academy to remove accent marks from Spanish printed materials upon Spain's entry to the European Economic Community. Implicit in this presentation is a call to the reader to prevent the occurrence of such a scenario.

The extent of U.S. influence on Mexico in 1992 becomes increasingly apparent in the Anglicization of place names. Mexico City becomes Make-sicko City, Mexico Seedy, Huitzilopochtliburg, Quasimodoville. The Indian culture at the heart of Mexican history and culture is trivialized in these names as well, as it bows to the imposition from the North. On the streets, the hip talk is Anglatl, a hybridization of English, Nahuatl, and Spanish. The future generation of Mexican leaders appropriates this modern jargon instead of perpetuating their own multicultural heritage through language.[9]

Leticia Reyes-Tatinclaux suggests that the decomposition of Mexico's language in the text expresses the disintegration of Mexico itself (p. 103). Certainly, the novel utilizes linguistic expression to underscore its thematic premise. The nation's undiscerning openness to foreign influence results not only in the creation of Mexamerica, but in the glib assimilation of English terminology and in a pathetic reintegration of the Indian language. There are serious repercussions to the erosion of a language that affect the cultural perceptions inherent in collective expression. Fuentes's picture of a future Mexico takes to extremes the initial signs of decay that he perceives as he writes.

In his inscription of various discourses, then, Carlos Fuentes unmasks the continual process of transformation that language undergoes. The novel exposes the structural fiber of Mexican culture and its institutions, media, and language. Naturally, as a postmodern writer Fuentes extends this examination to the text. In *Cristóbal Nonato*, the constructed nature of fiction is illustrated through intertextuality and through the conscious use and abuse of textual conventions.

Intertextuality has a dual function in the novel. The incorporation of other texts shows its indebtedness to them, and acknowledges the previously scripted status of fiction. Intertextual references are at times transformed, engendering an apocryphal version of events. The text of Kafka's *Metamorphosis* is inverted so that "un insecto despertó una mañana convertido en Franz Kafka." (p. 106) [An insect awoke one day, turned into Franz Kafka.] The implication fashions a concept of literature wherein texts refurbish one another, and where each reading transforms the text itself.[10]

Drawing on an international body of literature, Fuentes often incorporates references in the form of epigraphs or name insertions; he borrows characters or trademark phrases from other works. Thus, intertexuality perfoms its second function: it graphically, almost tangibly, illustrates the constructed nature of a text, pasting together pieces of a collage. Not only are the original references transformed, but they also become an apt vehicle for extending the text's associations beyond the written page in front of both author and reader. The text weaves a literary tapestry of cross-reference that breaks open the text to its parallel and intersecting planes of literature, and calls forth the individual experience of the reader to amplify the text of *Cristóbal Nonato*.

The sources of epigraphs range from Marx to López Velarde, the Mexican poet of the early twentieth century. As is customary in Fuentes, he also includes characters or their close counterparts from his own earlier works: Robles Chacón, Artemio Cruz, Aura. Less traditional is the incorporation of well-known phrases from other writers, lifted from preexisting literature with little alteration: Nabokov ("Confiesa mi padre caer rendido, ayer y hoy y mañana, ante niñas entre los tres y los trece años de edad," p. 125) [My father confesses he collapses—yesterday, today, and tomorrow—in the presence of girls between three and thirteen years of age. (p. 107)]; Ortega y Gasset ("Yo soy Cristóbal y mis circunstancias," p. 31) [I am Christopher plus my circumstance. (p. 6)]; García Márquez ("Hasta adquirí la costumbre heroicamente insana de hablar solo," p. 134); [I even acquired the insanely heroic habit of talking to myself. (p. 116)].

Fuentes incorporates figures from other literatures into the space of his narrative. This technique is foregrounded in *Terra Nostra*, when figures from a painting step off the canvas and into the narrative, sharing the same literary plane with the novel's own figures. In *Cristóbal Nonato*, Susana Rentería (a composite of characters from Juan Rulfo's novel) marries Angel's grandfather, fulfilling Pedro Páramo's dying wish that she be considered part of his purchased land.

The poetic evocation of López Velarde's Agueda (from "Mi prima Agueda"), a nostalgic childhood image tinged with sexual desire, is incorporated in Fuentes's novel somewhat differently. While Angel is in Oaxaca, a magical city whose very environment restores him, he comes upon Agueda in a small church. Perhaps the serenity of the supernatural triggers his fantasy: they caress and make love, but the spell is broken when he abruptly awakes the next morning, alone. It is unclear whether she is a figment of Angel's imagination or a "real" character; he wonders if she too responds to a fantasy of her own in coming to him. Regardless of the origin of Agueda's character, she does exist within the textual space of the novel; and it is relatively unimportant that her parentage is a literary construct. The significance of this form of intertextuality lies in its assumption that both fiction and reality are artificially constructed entities.

Conventional perceptions of reality are challenged in the novel as well. Niña Ba in *Cristóbal Nonato* illustrates the deficiency of our perceptions. To the other characters, she is an imaginary construct of the Huérfano Huerta: they accept his belief in her, but do not acknowledge her existence in their world. But she does interact with the group when the band plays: a fourth instrument, the piccolo, is heard when the three band members' hands and voices are occupied making music. It is as if Niña Ba exists on her own plane, trapped somehow within Huérfano's consciousness, only marginally accessible to his outer world through sound.

Cristóbal acknowledges Niña Ba's existence within the womb, and shares that fluid space with her. As he is being born, he asks that she come with him; she remains within the womb, however, underscoring her status as a character in potential. The hyperspace of the womb allows for her presumed existence. It will be the reader, perhaps, who will call her into another plane of existence: the text. Literature, then, is among the plural levels of reality, one of the myriads of which we may be unaware. The text might be considered a great, equalizing plane where mimesis, dreams, imagination, and the creative powers of language converge, creating a reality as "real" as that which is external to the text.

In another textual incident that exposes the constructed nature of reality, Angel's grandparents devise a money-saving system for catching mice, due to the exorbitant cost of setting cheese in the traps. They replace the cheese with a photograph of a piece of cheese; the next morning they find in its place a photograph of a mouse. When imitation replaces the original image, the simulacrum becomes real; as both Magritte and Baudrillard illustrated, although somewhat differently, the representation gains in ontological status through its fundamental operation.

The substitution of the real with signs of the real[11] points to a fundamental shift in the conceptualization of representation. In the instance cited above, the referent (cheese and mouse), previously grounded in an external reality and directly accessible through a specific linguistic sign, is twice removed from its original position. In the words of Baudrillard, "The representational imaginary . . . disappears with simulation. . . . It is no longer a question of imitation, nor of reduplication, nor even of parody. . . . It is nothing more than operational." (p. 3) The design of the text of Cristóbal Nonato underscores this premise.

Cristóbal exists within a timeless realm, and doesn't understand the concept of time: "Tiempo? qué es? cuándo empiezo a contar mi vida?" (p. 23) [Time? what is it? . . . when do I begin to count the days of my life? (p. 16)] However, Cristóbal adopts this artificial construct of the world beyond the womb and gives the ages of each character as they are introduced in the novel. The result is the underscoring of the superfluous nature of time, of an attempted imposition of order on a nonmeasurable notion. As his birth draws near, Cristóbal grows increasingly aware of the passing of time, developing a need to know when he will be born. His approach to the external world is signaled by his growing dependence on the construct of time.

In terms of textual authority, Fuentes dedicates much of *Cristóbal Nonato* to defying traditional concepts of the novel. The narrative premise is unlikely, if not impossible—it postulates an unborn, yet omniscient, entity. Cristóbal cannot exist as an all-knowing narrator outside the womb, therefore the narration necessarily ceases with his birth.

The role of the reader, particularly, undergoes transformation as he acquires a rare independence from narrative control. Not only does the narrator initiate dialogue with and address him directly, but the reader is given the name "Elector," combining his two functions: he is asked both to choose and to read, and thus to participate in finishing the details of the plot. Elector transgresses the lines of authorship as his participation becomes integral to the plot. He is asked to fill in a blank page to his liking, and towards the end of the novel he selects from a number of options and concludes the plot.

Traditional reader expectations are stretched and sometimes mocked. On several occasions, Fuentes constructs a scene that seems to lead towards a climactic revelation, only to announce: "No, aquí no va a haber revelación melodramática." (p. 472) [No, there will be no melodramatic revelations here. (p. 445)] His frequent use of direct address to the reader allows for an occasional goading of the reader in the best propagandist style: "Dénles ustedes sus destinos, s.v.p.! Esta novela es de ustedes, señores electores!" (p. 513) [You give them their destinies, svp! This novel belongs to you, dear Readers! (p. 483)]

Toward the end of the novel, Cristóbal's urgency increases as he addresses the reader to remind him of his indispensable place in the creation of the narrative: "Tú sabes, elector, que sin ti no me habría salido con la mía, que es comunicarles a los vivos mis pesadillas y mis sueños: ahora ya son *sus* pesadillas y *sus* sueños." (p. 551) [You know, Reader, that without you I would not have done what I want, which is to communicate to the living my nightmares and my dreams. (p. 519)] Fuentes thus continues the principle established in *Una familia lejana* (1980). Reiterating the postmodern notion of endings that do not end, the reader's continuation of the text makes definitive conclusions impossible.

Other elliptical moments within the text subvert the notion of one definitive version of events. The disaster of Acapulco is purported to be the doing first of the Four Jodiditos, then of the guerrillas, and finally we are told that the government authorized the guerrillas to wreak havoc on the city. We are led to believe that both Homero and Penny López died, but they later reappear in the novel with plausible reasons for their survival. The hysteron-proteron trope is often inscribed in *Cristóbal Nonato*, undermining the reader's need for causality. Fuentes engages the readers in a playful dialogue with the text itself, providing them with enough clues to give the impression of causality, yet often disrupting their logic.

The author's authority is discredited on the grounds that he lacks the final word on the form and content of the text. The text itself, paradoxically, both gains and loses autonomy in this act. The loss of control by both author and reader over narrative elements—plot, ending, traditionally rigid associations of linguistic signs—would imply that the text can stand on its own, an entity rich in meaning and unlimited potential for recombination. At the same time, however, the reduction of the text to its components conveys a vulnerability to manipulation by a creative power. Just as the elements of language take on meaning through the relationships that are imposed upon them, in Fuentes's view the text comes into being as it is read, as the associations laid out in nontraditional form give way to new possibilities of existence. What remains after reading Fuentes's novel is a linguistic artifact that has been crafted self-consciously. The extreme self-reflexivity of *Cristóbal Nonato* thus lends itself to the postmodern aim of exposing the constructed nature of fiction.

The novel also deconstructs myth in order to subvert its authority as a collective, accepted script. Ulises's wife does not remain faithful to him when he leaves in his quest for economic gain and political success. Rather, it is his daughter, named Penelope, who spurns her suitors while Lucha aggressively seeks them out. In the postmodern world, nothing can be assumed to follow a predetermined pattern.

Fuentes both exploits and inverts traditional Christian symbolism in *Cristóbal Nonato*. Angel and Angeles both demonstrate a sense of otherworldliness as they separate themselves from the immediate to consider the past as well as the future, momentarily participating in the timeless realm of the angels. Angeles, eight months pregnant, rides into her Bethlehem on a donkey, whereupon she and Angel are raped and beaten by Matamoros Moreno, recalling Jesus' suffering after Golgotha. As a cult figure, Matamoros Moreno adopts a messianic stance in his proclamation of salvation to the Mexican truck drivers during his ill-fated religious campaign. He dies a sacrificial lamb, his life offered in exchange for that of the truckers. This Mexican messiah rewrites the Sermon on the Mount as he reenacts the Christian myth.

The figure of Mamadoc represents in part the Virgin Mary, and inspires fervent religious devotion among the populace. From the Protestant camp, the Reverend Royall Payne embodies a curious mixture of Southern fundamentalism in his flamboyant tele-vangelism, and Old Testament militancy in conceiving of the battle as an equally spiritual and national venture.

The Christian sacrament of baptism is juxtaposed with the Aztec myth of the scatological origin of the gods. In a final syn-thesis, the cathedral becomes the scene of sexual encounter for Angel on two occasions—first with Agueda, then upon his recon-ciliation with Angeles. Although the institutionalized forms of religion have failed—Capitolina and Farnesia's barren Catholi-cism, Matamoros Moreno's violent fanaticism, and Reverend Payne's glitzy fundamentalism—there is still cause for optimism in individual expressions of devotion and charity. Angel and Angeles choose to love each other, and to raise their son in Mex-ico. Again, the implications of this discovery extend to the collective.

From his womb's view, Cristóbal is aided by the wisdom of centuries contained in his genes; it is a knowledge that he will forget at birth and spend his life trying to regain. However, there is hope that he will in fact eventually remember; this is true particularly because of the revised mentality of his parents. Angel and Angeles are representative of a new generation of Mexicans who wonder about the future of their nation. Although she has no past (she knows neither her parents nor her birth date), Angeles asks the most practical questions concerning her son's future—questions that remain ultimately unresolved but that indicate an awareness of the current crises in Mexico. That awareness holds potential for this generation's coming to terms with their responsibility for the outcome of 1992 and beyond.

Angel's choosing to remain in Mexico, instead of succumbing to the temptation of Pacífica, an Oriental utopia, indicates a re-newed commitment to the possibilities within Mexico's future. Potentially the shared experience of others in his generation, Angel's review of the past has provided him with a future. Ange-les is without a past and can begin the present unburdened; she must fashion her own past within the present. For this woman of practical concerns, as well, the considerations of culture and its directions, as manifested by its past, grant her the opportunity of a hopeful future.

The postmodern satirical mode employed in Cristóbal Nonato provides a novelistic construction that subverts narrative convention. As a result, the self-reflexive statements of the text reveal the artificiality of discourse and demythify traditional agents of control. Although the novel does not provide a whole, restored vision of any of Mexico's institutions, the cultural critique manifested on various levels in the text allows for a reduction of Mexico to its essence. As readers, we participate in the civic duty of choosing a destiny for our children, acting today to change the world in which they will live. This action is necessarily accompanied by an examination of history.

The novel provides an illustration of human agency in history. Because key structuring elements are left deliberately ambiguous, the reader plays a significant role in the formation of the text. Cristóbal's fate—What language will he speak?—remains unresolved. The scripted nature of reality and literature, coupled with the absence of a guaranteed future (judging by the physical situation before us) demands of the reader that she consider her own reality. In his projection of Mexico's future, Fuentes has inevitably looked to its past for an understanding of the forces that are shaping its present. Following in the postmodern vein, he has also examined the present to gain perspective on history. The subjectified nature of time leads to subjective versions of history. What is current imposes its view on what is past; no historical event is concluded by the simple passage of time. It fluctuates along with the varying considerations of history.

As the next chapter discusses, Fuentes turns his attention to this aspect of history. Our study will appropriately involve the novels immediately preceding and immediately following Cristóbal Nonato, thus illustrating the cyclical motion of history that frequently makes its appearance in Fuentes's writing. The present rewriting of history poses certain problems in the textual representation of the subjectified realms of memory, consciousness, and dreaming. The construct of fiction becomes an appropriate vehicle for the exploration of the construct of history.

5

Reconsiderations of the Past: *Gringo viejo* (1985) and *La campaña* (1990)

CARLOS FUENTES CONSISTENTLY INCORPORATES THE HISTORICAL REFerent in his works, yet in two of his most recent fictions, *Gringo viejo* (1985) and *La campaña* (1990), history performs a different function. Novels prior to *Terra Nostra* show the dynamic relationship between temporal zones, illustrating primarily the influence of the past on the present. Post-1975 novels press this notion further to include a radicalization of the concept of time and, utilizing accurate historical contexts, rewrite the past with a measure of self-reflexivity that characterizes them as postmodern works of historiographic metafiction. In *Gringo viejo* and *La campaña*, Fuentes gives full expression to the postmodern view of history and its representation.

Postmodernism regards history as a discursive medium much like fiction, which as such must be considered a subjective construct.[1] Departing from the changes in perception of historiography as articulated by Hayden White, Linda Hutcheon proposes that the events of the past are converted into fact by discursive structuring, more than by any objective standard.[2] She terms this change in the documentation of history a shift from validation to signification (p. 191), signaling a postmodern awareness of the constructed nature of the telling of the past, based on narrative positioning of events and characters. The question is no longer which version is true, but what factors shape each telling.

In historiographic metafiction, narrative positioning allows a disruptive ordering of the events of the past. Retrospective narration is replaced by "anonymous forces of dissipation. . . . Contradictions replace totalities; discontinuities, gaps, and ruptures are favored in opposition to continuity, development, evolution; the particular and the local take on the value once held by the universal and transcendent."[3] In *Gringo viejo*, for example, the important events of the Mexican Revolution—particular battles and figures such as Pancho Villa and Obregón—occupy the periphery of the plot, while such ex-centrics as the Old Gringo and his burning of the fictive Arroyo's land titles move to its center.

The extreme self-reflexivity of historiographic metafiction facilitates the overt subversion of traditional practices of writing about the past. It consciously bears little resemblance to Lukács's historical novel that Hutcheon discusses. The representative microcosms in historiographic metafiction are generally peopled with "improper" types who are marginal to society. Like Pynchon's "second sheep" in *Gravity's Rainbow*, some of Fuentes's protagonists are unlikely to achieve greatness: in *Gringo viejo*, a spinster from Washington, D.C., goes to Mexico hoping to add meaning to her life; in *La campaña*, a spy in the Independence movement dies not as a hero, but rather of cancer. These figures move from the periphery to occupy, for a moment in fiction, centralized roles.

The traditional historical novel's incorporation of historical personages in secondary roles attempts to validate its fictional world, hiding the seams between fiction and history.[4] The postmodern historical novel, by contrast, attempts to expose this and other ordering patterns latent in the text. The problem of how we know reality at all is foregrounded; we also ask what is the nature of the realities we encounter. This epistemological and ontological questioning is compounded in historiographic metafiction by the perception that all previous history is scripted: the details of a particular account have already been arranged to corroborate a chosen emphasis, embedded in the events that are warranted as factual. The presence of historical data in postmodern texts serves more often to problematize its significance, rather than to underscore an ideological premise. Historiographic metafiction makes its task the unveiling of ideological presuppositions behind discourse.

Finally, the issue of subjectivity in the postmodern recording of history is enacted textually through multiple, dissenting points of view or by an overly controlling narrator whose very imposition of perspective undermines his or her authority. The result is a narrative stance that is subverted from within. The textual presentation of actual historical events is, therefore, also called into question. We return to the issue of reliability and "truth" of historical documentation, as well as to that of authorship.

La campaña and *Gringo viejo* are works of historiographic metafiction in that they manifest a self-reflexive narrative positioning of historical events. Although their methods differ, the end is common to both novels: to recount history in a way that exposes the traditionally undisclosed assumptions behind the historical text. The result extends beyond a refutation of historical fiction to the establishment of new ordering and dis-ordering structures that enrich our reading of history.

Both novels make it clear that the narrators are recounting events from an earlier time; relating the past from a current perspective underscores the recent nature of historical accounts. This factor alone prompts the reader to the awareness that this is a constructed version of events, molded in part by whatever influences are being exerted upon the narrative process. Each version is therefore suspect, since its rendering involves a number of suppositions that are unaccounted for.

Gringo viejo records the process of recalling visions from the past. The irrationality of dreams and memory interrupts the external chronology of historical events, invariably rearranging the sequence of events and inverting the measure of their importance. Consequently, a new version of history emerges. Although *La campaña* evokes the past somewhat differently, it also aims to show the subjectivity of any historical account. The novel is structured to highlight the narrator's motivations in ordering his account, emphasizing some events and suppressing others. The intentional exposure of such processes problematizes the issue of objectivity in historical texts.

This carries significant implications for the reader, who must consequently examine a plurality of truths in the present retelling of history. Ultimately, the reader's uncertainty as to which version is definitive—what actually occurred—is a conscious intent of these texts. Different historical accounts may vie with each other, but none of them represents the totality of past experience. Fuentes intends to demonstrate, through this final irresolution, the constructed nature of history itself. As works of historiographic metafiction, *Gringo viejo* and *La campaña* explore Fuentes's own subversive rendering of the past.

Gringo viejo constructs a fictional ending to Ambrose Bierce's life. Fuentes bases his story on the turn-of-the-century Anglo misanthrope and journalist who, at the age of seventy-one, goes to Mexico to die. He seeks to die proving himself to be a brave man and envisions his death before a Mexican firing squad.

Fuentes begins his account of this man's last days with his entrance into Mexico, crossing the border in El Paso after buying a horse and riding into the desert in search of Pancho Villa's revolutionary forces. He finds a group of them led by General Tomás Arroyo, the bastard son of a wealthy landlord by the name of Miranda who has just fled the country with his family. The band of rebels arrives at the Miranda hacienda and destroys it completely, sparing only the mirrored walls of the dance hall. There they encounter Harriet Winslow, a thirty-one-year-old schoolteacher from Washington who has come to teach the Miranda children. She completes the novel's triangle of characters, along with General Arroyo and the Old Gringo.

The characters involve themselves in conflicting relationships: Harriet is drawn to the virility of the Mexican general and to the fatherly affection of the Old Gringo; he oscillates between passion and paternal feelings for Harriet; Arroyo's attraction to Harriet potentially represents a role reversal of U.S. domination. When the conflicts come to a head, the Old Gringo burns Arroyo's papers of land ownership, inciting the general to kill him; Pancho Villa orders the Gringo disinterred and shot before a firing squad, and does the same with Arroyo; and Harriet returns to Washington with the Gringo's body, claiming it as her missing father's.

Fuentes places the narrative within the context of the Mexican Revolution but his focus is not the legendary heroes such as Pancho Villa, but the secondary, fictional figures that he creates. The novel's treatment of history is shaped by the subjectification of time and the inclusion of dreams and memory. Simultaneity, acausality, and diachronicity pattern the events of the novel; this facilitates the novel's shift to the hidden, silent activity of the internal realm. A subjective ordering of events thus takes place, as *Gringo viejo* aims to incorporate this undocumented activity—of memory, thoughts, desires, and dreams—in its creation of fictionalized history.

Much of the narration takes place in Harriet Winslow's mind as she remembers, now back in her apartment in Washington, the events of her stay in Mexico. Thus, the majority of the novel is recalled; however, within this framework occurs a series of digressions. The flashback is not subsequently chronological, nor is it uncommon for the narration to skip back to the present time, and in and out of the minds of other characters. This is significant to the whole ambience of timelessness and to the projection of the world of thoughts, imagination, and dreams as being limitless, lacking boundaries between the imaginary and the real. Likewise, this world does not have barriers between the minds of its characters.

Digressions occur in the form of fragments of conversations, of openings into the mental activity of various characters, and of the recounting of events by other characters. These conversations do not follow typical dialogue fashion; they are reduced to one or two lines by each speaker, their exchanges separated by sometimes extensive recordings of thoughts or later reflections. The speakers, seldom identified, contribute to a sense of the blurring and disappearing of lines between the world of reality and the world of dreams. The readers are subjected to feelings of uncertainty as they lose their footing in a marsh of disappearing conventions of time, space, and a clear distinction between dreams and reality.

Gringo viejo makes tangible the experience of dreaming and remembering through a series of well-executed images. Narration of the nonexternal is consistently prefigured in the novel by references to smoke, fog, or dust, reminiscent of early cinematic blurring of the image on the screen to signal a flashback or a dream. Light and dark play off each other, and Harriet's memories of her father are recalled in images of a dank basement. This realm is spoken of as labyrinths, descending ladders, and mirrors that split repeatedly. The physicalization of mental processes facilitates the reader's apprehension of this activity.

The central image of the internal realm is that of the mirrored walls of the Miranda dance hall. Harriet Winslow's refracted image symbolizes the breaking of an Anglo-American, puritanical, works-oriented philosophy, an elementary step in bringing her to an awareness of and eventual participation in this dream-like world. In contrast, the Mexican soldiers who see themselves in a mirror for the first time are amazed to see their perceived diversity of self reduced to an integral corporeal unity.

The novel exploits the polarities of Mexican and U.S. culture with regard to the importance assigned to internal, subjective realities. Fuentes thus politicizes his depiction of seen/unseen and temporal/atemporal experiences. The implication is that Mexicans move daily in a world that acknowledges the imagined, and that bases itself on the interaction of the seen and the unseen. It is their way of life that empowers Harriet eventually to carry with her the memory of the Old Gringo and Arroyo, to call it forth after returning to her apartment in Washington, allowing her to perceive their "mobilized pasts." This constitutes a kind of cultural victory over U.S. hegemony, one that serves the theme of the Revolution well.

Essentially, the world of dreams in the novel is separate from the real one; dreams are nonetheless inextricably woven in and through what we normally consider "real." No longer depicted as peripheral to the world of objectified activity, the world of dreams becomes a powerful, rupturing force:

> Pero volvería a dormir, volvería a soñar: la ruptura de los sueños en la máquina minutera que todos los días destruía el verdadero tiempo interno en la molienda de la actividad, sólo le daba un relieve mayor, un valor más acentuado, al mundo del instante eterno, que regresaría de noche, mientras ella dormía y soñaba sola.
> [But she would sleep again, she would dream again: dream's interruption of the minute hand that daily grinds away true internal time in the mill of activity merely emphasizes, and intensifies, the world of the eternal instant that would return by night, while she slept and dreamed alone.][5]

The realm of dreams is free from temporal conventions and the other world is not; yet the nature of dreams is the nature of true time. Capable of calling into being both what is dead and what is forgotten, dreams perpetuate life, thus asserting the superiority of the internal over the external.

Dreams maintain a tangible proximity to real life. In the novel, a thought or memory intensifies to such a degree of vividness that it becomes a dream: "Pensé mucho en ti anoche. Estuviste muy vívida en mis pensamientos. Creo que hasta soñé contigo." (p. 99) ["I thought a lot about you last night. You were very real in my thoughts. I think I even dreamed about you. (p. 103)] The equalization of the internal and external planes casts doubt on previous assumptions of an objectified, reliable separation of the two, following the postmodern hesitancy in fiction to differentiate between reality and fantasy.

At one point, the Old Gringo steps into Harriet Winslow's room and finds her sleeping. He impulsively kisses her on the cheek. He wishes her dream could last as long and even longer than the war and Mexico, and that they could somehow join dreams afterward. As his lips press against her cheek, he absorbs the whole of her dream and of her subconscious. It all takes place in an instant and with his eyes open, substantiating the compenetration of reality and dreams.

In another instance, Harriet Winslow's conscience leaps into Arroyo's head: "La conciencia fragmentada de Harriet Winslow dio un salto en el vacío para meterse en la cabeza del General Tomás Arroyo." (p. 144) [Harriet Winslow's fragmented consciousness leapt through the void into the mind of General To-

más Arroyo. (p. 162)] Arroyo too, as if by some psychic process
of osmosis, assimilates the dreams of his men so that he knows,
without their expressing it, what they are thinking: "Claro que
Arroyo soñó todo esto, o lo supo porque sus hombres lo so-
ñaron." (p. 89) [Certainly Arroyo dreamed these things, or knew
them because his men dreamed them. (p. 90)] The lack of boundaries separating the subjective activities of others depicts a fluid,
internal realm, and reasserts its significance to the world of the
external.

Even intuition is transcendent when a person's thoughts skip
over the verbal, objective realm and go directly to another's inner
reality. Fuentes captures this process in the following passage:

> Ya no oyó lo que añadió Arroyo (Es un rejego. Es valiente. Es una
> mala cosa para mi tropa ser así) sino lo que no añadió (No pasaré
> esta noche sin ti. Te deseo como no te imaginas, gringuita. . . . Perdó-
> name pero haré lo que sea para tenerte esta noche, gringuita
> preciosa).
>
> (p. 109)
>
> [She didn't hear what Arroyo added (He's stubborn. He's a brave
> man. And he's a bad example to my men) but what he did not add
> (I won't spend this night without you. I want you, more than you can
> imagine, little gringa. . . . Forgive me, but I will do whatever I have
> to do to have you tonight, my beautiful gringa.]
>
> (p. 113)

When the Old Gringo speaks of the restoration of dreams that
will take place due to the role of memory, he is touching upon
yet another component of this inner world. To remember something in this novel does much more than call forth a distant
event, emotion, act, odor, person, or impression: it constitutes a
reality of its own. It is the creation of another reality within the
present one, activated by remembering. Each re-creation has its
own, separate identity. This is true as well of the products of the
interior realm in *Gringo viejo*, whether it is a dream, a thought,
or a memory.

The Old Gringo's conscience speaks directly to him on one
occasion and asks whether or not he realizes that Harriet Winslow has been creating him, just as he has been creating her.
"¿Sabías que todos somos objeto de la imaginación ajena?"
(p. 138) [Did you know we are all objects of another's imagination? (p. 143)] The second reality of the imagination creates concrete realities in the inner realm of things. These separate
realities temporarily converge to form a broader plane that in-

cludes both creators' artifacts. Their union, localized in hyper-space, is however only momentary.

From the moment of Harriet Winslow's entrance into the dream world as she enters the hall of mirrors, her conscience is shown to be split as she dreams of new realities, as her mind explores the unfamiliar, and as she attempts to divorce her soul from her body. Her view of the Old Gringo is fragmented as well, since she is for a time unsure of whether she sees him as a father or as a lover. From his perspective, the conflicting image is of a similar nature. There is, however, one instance when the divided halves of these two characters meet, creating in that union a regained semblance of a whole inner being for each of them.

This moment occurs immediately before the Old Gringo's death at the hand of General Tomás Arroyo. Harriet Winslow and the Old Gringo find themselves together, airing their true feelings for the first and last time. Whereas before, the Old Gringo has kissed her on the cheek, he now kisses her on the mouth, and sees her as he has imagined her. In a sense, then, the reality of the mind comes to fruition at this moment:

> Harriet miró al gringo viejo como al gringo le hubiera gustado ser visto antes de morir. El gringo sintió que esa mirada completó la secuencia fragmentada de su imaginación de Harriet Winslow, abierta por los reflejos de los espejos del salón de baile que sólo eran el umbral de un camino al sueño, atomizado en mil instantes oníricos y ahora reunido de nuevo en las palabras.
>
> (p. 142)
>
> [Harriet looked at the old gringo exactly as he wanted to be looked at before he died. He felt that her gaze completed the fragmented sequence of his imagination of Harriet Winslow that had begun in the reflections of the mirrors in the ballroom that was but a threshold of the road to dream, atomized into a thousand oneiric instants and now joined again in words.]
>
> (p. 149)

This results in the creation of a magical, timeless entity that is as short-lived as it is intense. Diverse elements of each character's reality suddenly converge and synthesize the whole of the character's existence. It is as if one person's inner and external realities are floating, fragmented, in indeterminate relationship. Piece by piece the reader is provided with fragments of the characters—a thought, a dialogue, a memory, a briefly exposed subconscious, a physical description—and for us as readers the characters come into existence as these images coagulate, then shift, then dissolve as we move across the pages of the novel. The internal and the external, then, are treated as equally textual and are equally woven into the surface of Fuentes's fiction.

"Ella se sienta sola y recuerda." [She sits alone and remembers.] The repeated insertion of this phrase in the narration draws attention to the solitary nature of remembering. In her apartment in Washington, separated from her experiences in Mexico by both temporal and spatial distances, Harriet restores the past "como un argumento largo, poblado de detalles, de arquitecturas y de incidentes." (p. 57) [as an elaborate plot peopled with details, structures, and incidents. (p. 52)] Within her own consciousness she calls forth a myriad of elements from the past, restructuring them as one would a plot. In a postmodern illustration of the constructed nature of the past, Harriet's Mexican venture is reformed in the instant of evocation. The possibility of recombination of events is seemingly endless and allows for different emphases. The sections introduced by this phrase shift the narrative to center on a previously undisclosed aspect of her story, as if reference to the unseen, inner realm of activity would alter the reader's impression of events. The reconstruction of her past necessarily repositions the elements of her story. The same is true of any recounting of the past, whether termed "history" or "fiction."

Subverting the hierarchy of importance that has been established by "objective" historical accounts, the central becomes peripheral in the *Gringo viejo*. The drama of the Mexican Revolution serves merely as a backdrop to the Gringo's plan. History becomes an agent for the fulfillment of an individual's wish to die in front of a Mexican firing squad, rather than being the guiding force that determines his death.

Conversely, the novel's postmodern rearrangement of hierarchy provisionally repositions the marginal to the center. Similarly to *La campaña*, the novel focuses not on the abundance of legendary figures from the Revolution, but on the "second sheep" or on previously scripted figures. It is interesting that Fuentes chooses Bierce, a figure narrativized by his biographers, on which to construct his own textual character. In this shift of emphasis to the nonhistorical, the action of the novel moves further from the centralized hierarchy of traditional historical accounts. As mentioned previously, the Old Gringo's burning of the papers is a central event in the novel; his action culminates one series of conflicts and sets off another. Fuentes thus positions centrally a fictional incident within the objective events of the Mexican Revolution.

This ordering principle is common to historical fiction—it affords a voice to the author's particular emphasis in telling his version of events. Fuentes's use of this principle, making the peripheral a part of the historical canon, underscores the plotting devices common to both historiography and fiction. His exposure of the fictional plotting of history reveals the subjectivity of this procedure, and consequently subverts the notion of historical accuracy and truth.

Additionally, Harriet's process of remembering structures the narrative in a nonlinear sequence of events. The novel's first scene describes the disinterring of the Old Gringo, but the subsequent narration is not reversely chronological. Rather, as in *La muerte de Artemio Cruz*, the sequencing follows its own, internal logic. Causal order is restored only in the reader's mind. *Gringo viejo* thus subverts traditional notions of time, promoting instead a conceptualization of the past that includes a nonlinear temporality, with an enlarged field of activity that acknowledges the role of dreams and memory. The undermining of causality, and the repositioning of events of a temporal hierarchy that presumes to be objective, present other possibilities of relationship.

The mixture of fact and fiction remains a problematic issue in historical fiction. Fuentes addresses this in his 1985 novel, utilizing intertextuality to yield further indeterminacy to the historical account by calling attention to its reconstruction based in part on parallel texts, not on objective historical data. Ambrose Bierce becomes a fictional character once he enters Mexico, since the details of the journalist's death are unknown. Fuentes reconstructs a possible death, drawing up an architectural plan that plots a synchronization of narrative elements: character, time, and place. The result is one typical of historical fiction, except for one significant factor: Fuentes includes only occasional references to Ambrose Bierce; he does not let the reader forget that his character is not Bierce himself but rather the Old Gringo. This represents a disruption of traditional readings that accept the historicity of a novel that situates itself within a historically accurate context. The reader is reminded by Fuentes that she is reading a fiction, not a "true" account, by this pulling apart of the historical person from the fictional character.

Fuentes also includes references, both overt and hidden, to Bierce's own writing.[6] The Old Gringo quotes as his own several of Bierce's satiric definitions from *The Devil's Dictionary;* these references thus serve to characterize the Old Gringo and evoke the callousness of Bierce as the literary figure: the bitterness of Bierce's life and his tardy recognition of his wrongdoing explain the Old Gringo's wish to die. The intertextual references thereby emphasize the narrativized quality of this historical account.

As Joseph Chrzanowski and Joaquín Roy have shown, several scenes in *Gringo viejo* have been appropriated, with little alteration, from Bierce's fiction. The narrative calls this fact to the reader's attention: "Aquí se estaba volviendo realidad fantasmal un cuento." (p. 60) [a story was becoming a ghostly reality. (p. 56)] In addition, the theme of patricide is evident in both Fuentes's text and the stories of Bierce that are referred to in the novel. Once again, Fuentes's use of intertextuality carries with it an implicit questioning of levels of reality and fictionality.

To reveal that a historical novel's sources borrow from other fictions, and not from direct experience or first-hand accounts, is to severely discredit the veracity of historical writing. Fuentes's self-reflexivity presents this process of data-collecting as storymaking, and presents internal and external events as equally important. The subjectification of the process of historical reconstruction solidly situates *Gringo viejo* within historiographic metafiction, and presents a serious questioning of any construct that presents itself as objectively historical.

La campaña (1990) remakes history in its evocation of the South-American Independence movements of the early nineteenth century. The novel creates literary characters who participate in historically documented events, dividing the action of the novel between Buenos Aires, the Andean highlands of Perú, Santiago, Maracaibo, and Veracruz. This account documents the revolutionary fervor that rocked the continent from top to bottom, ending with the protagonist's brief encounter with the initial stirring of Mexican independence. The South American hero, José de San Martín, figures marginally in the narration as Baltasar's commanding general, and Simón Bolívar even less, mentioned by name only occasionally. The novel's postmodern treatment of history figures both in its narrative presentation and in its treatment of the mythic conventions that structure the text.

The narrator immediately identifies himself as Manuel Varela, an Argentine *criollo* like his companions, Xavier Dorrego and Baltasar Bustos. On the eve of Argentine independence, they are disciples of Rousseau, steeped in the ideals of the Enlightenment. In support of the revolution, Baltasar takes justice into his own hands and switches the President's wife's baby with a black child. A fire breaks out and the black child is killed; no one knows of the attempted change of fate, and the lesson of social equality goes unlearned. Baltasar's naive assumptions about the execution of justice thus end in tragedy, and he flees Buenos Aires, returning to his father's estate on the pampa. Shortly thereafter he joins the rebel forces, embarking on a ten-year campaign in pursuit of political freedom for his continent, civil justice, and a personal passion for Ofelia, the Argentine President's wife. Varela and Dorrego remain in Buenos Aires collecting clocks, reading Baltasar's letters, and awaiting his return, virtually at a standstill, as if their lives cannot not advance until the threesome is restored.

Utilizing the conventions of realism, the narrator gives an account in the limited omniscience of an objective observer. Varela is a printer by profession, and although it is implied, it is not revealed until the end of the novel that the text is an account based on the collection of Baltasar's letters to Varela and Dorrego. Similarly to the narration of *Gringo viejo*, Varela bases his own account on one that has been previously scripted. This revelation also admits that Varela has had a hand in recording, if not altering, these events.

Varela himself alludes to this ironically in his comment about one of Baltasar's letters: "El círculo de lo escrito se cerraba sobre sus autores, capturándolos en la notable ficción de su propia inventiva: lo escrito es real y nosotros somos sus autores." [Thus, the circle of the written closed over its authors, capturing them in the noble fiction of their own inventive powers: the written is the real and we are its authors.][7] Varela's motivation comes from the undisclosed fact—revealed only in the novel's final pages—that he is the father of Ofelia's child. It is clear that this secret potentially causes Varela to write the text differently than the letters are structured, although he maintains an objective, third-person narrative stance, thereby showing how all "histories" are motivated discourses. *La campaña*, then, might be considered the "events" that Varela records as historical fact, excluding or modifying data when necessary in order to serve his own purposes.

Certainly, Varela never allows his readers to ignore his role as medium in the writing of the text. He frequently refers to his and Dorrego's reactions to Baltasar's letters: "Reirían sus amigos Dorrego y yo, Varela." (p. 49) [Said his friends, Dorrego and I, Varela, laughing. (p. 43)] He points to his presence with first-person references in a purportedly objective, third-person account, thus pointing to the covert dynamics of narration.

The text is riddled with phrases that contribute to a sense of uncertainty as to the "truth" of the novel. Varela sometimes contradicts himself: "Mis ojos casi claros (en realidad no lo son)" (p. 13) [my almost light (they really aren't) eyes. (p. 5)]; and he trivializes what has previously been established as significant: "Esperaba este momento, o uno parecido, para liberarte de aquí." (p. 191) ["I was waiting for this moment, or for one like it, to free you from this place. (p. 195)] The narrator's subversion of his own narration does great damage to a belief in textual veracity, and seems to once again demand an acknowledgement of the presence of a controlling, determining force, even behind an "objective" rendering of events. What ultimately remains is the narrative voice, but not his version of events.

Fuentes effectively undermines Varela's credibility as narrator, setting him on a self-destructive path. His vacillating commentary and obvious partiality in structuring events to maintain his secret lead to an inevitable discounting of his truth as objective. By extension, Varela's account of Baltasar's life can be only one of many. This self-discrediting narration, then, subverts the traditional foundations of historical fiction.

The installation and subversion of the conventions of myth perform a similar function in Fuentes's novel. History, as an achieved consensus about events that is imposed as fact, parallels myth in its imposition of the specifics of culture as natural, collective archetype. Both history and myth are ordered in retrospect, placing emphasis on a particular element or event in order to structure a desired outcome. La campaña exposes the process of myth-making by following the mythic journey, for instance, and then collapsing this pattern with a disruptively antithetical or fallen model. The result is not an antimyth or an antihero, which would qualify the novel as a modernist venture, but rather a text that utilizes mythic conventions self-reflexively to disclose its nature as a construct, and thus undermines its archetypal authority.

Baltasar figures as the unlikely candidate to embark on a mythic journey complete with a trip to the underworld, a timely meeting with several guides, trials that test his moral fiber, the return to an awaiting Penelope, and the eventual heroizing of the victorious, returning figure. In contrast to the traditional hero, Baltasar is indecisive, naive, bookish, and overweight, a man who spends ten years questioning the very cause for which he fights, attempting unsuccessfully (following Rousseau's prescriptions) to make himself one with nature. The origin of Baltasar's name is ironic: this "Owner of Treasure" does not possess, but only pursues his elusive treasure, represented by Ofelia.

His departure from Buenos Aires, as we have noted, comes as the result of a botched attempt to institute a new level of equal justice to society. Thus his departure is in flight from, not in response to, a call. Baltasar's decision to join the rebel cause is potentially an act of courage and nobility except that, as he himself recognizes, his decision is the result of his father's manipulation, which invalidates this act as a true show of strength. Furthermore, Baltasar is drafted and therefore forced to fight, his autonomy wrested from him. Similarly, the glorious battles and their stratagems find their scattered counterparts in the individualized tactics of the guerrillas in the Peruvian highlands.

Early on in his campaign, Baltasar visits the underworld in the form of the legendary city of lights, Eldorado. Guided by the mestizo, Simón Rodríguez, he descends into an intellectualized cave of sorts where his senses are transformed by the idea, not the sense, of light and sight. Baltasar is overwhelmed by what he sees: a city composed entirely of light, and a vision of Ofelia. She speaks to him not in the ageless wisdom of goddesses, but in a tone of spent regret: "No me mandes flores. Las odio. Y piensa de mí lo que quieras." (p. 89) ["Don't send me flowers. I hate them. And think what you like about me." (p. 87)] In its negativity, this depiction of Ofelia harmonizes with Shakespeare's character by the same name. Both women portray extreme suffering: Fuentes's figure loses her husband, her son, and her health; Shakespeare's character is driven mad by Hamlet's treatment of her and eventually commits suicide.

As he leaves the cave, Baltasar is convinced that he has witnessed the origin of man, perhaps sharing the thoughts of his Biblical namesake at the scene of Christ's birth. Baltasar is crestfallen that this genesis did not proceed in the least from a harmonious marriage of Man and Nature, as Rousseau had envisioned. Rather, it is a horrific mixture of life and death that stuns Baltasar. The guide realizes he has revealed too great a knowledge to his disciple: "Emplearía el resto de sus días tratando de olvidar la visión excepcional que nadie quería compartir, porque era incómoda, porque ponía en entredicho nuestras propias convicciones racionales." (p. 90) [[He would] . . . spend the rest of his days trying to forget this extraordinary vision that no one wanted to share, because it was disconcerting, because it put our own

rational convictions into doubt. (p. 88)] Instead of appropriating
the wisdom gained from this sacred vision, Baltasar spends his
life repudiating it.

Baltasar encounters three other guides as he continues his
journey. In a continued subverting of tradition, the first and last
are unorthodox priests, and the central one is a prostitute. Lutecia is the widow-turned-prostitute, in whose brothel Baltasar
faces a trial of compassion. He displays an unusual concern for
the sick in the hospital and even for Lutecia herself, who rewards
Baltasar by pointing him to his third guide, the Mexican Father, Quintana.

Quintana is a caricature of the wise man of fables: he sits at a
table, in contemplation of two identical bottles, trying to intuit
which is the evil wine and which is the good. Baltasar deduc-
tively reasons that this must be the man he is looking for; this
reasoning process and the proverb at the end of the episode
strongly suggest a parody of the medieval *exemplum*.

A guerrilla leader in the Mexican struggle for independence,
Quintana knows himself to be a guide for his people. When Baltasar confesses his life's wrongdoing, Quintana inverts the me-
diatory role of a Catholic priest and insists on confessing his
own sins to Baltasar. Both the priest and the layman experience
a cathartic purging of burdensome sin. This mentor's ready shift
from guiding to guided subverts the mythic conventions of im-
parting and seeking wisdom.

The prize to which Quintana leads Baltasar is Ofelia, the object
of his obsession since he first observed her sitting naked in front
of a mirror. Her beauty is described in the lofty, idealizing terms
of Renaissance and Baroque poetry. However, the image Baltasar
encounters when he finally lays eyes on her after ten years of
pursuit is that of an aged, cancer-stricken woman. Nearing death
and silenced by her suffering, Ofelia represents an impoverished
boon for Baltasar. Ultimately, he is denied even this version of
Ofelia, and is gifted with her son instead. Having captured the
prize, he now returns home to Buenos Aires.

Awaiting Baltasar are his friends, Varela and Dorrego, his figurative Penelope. The two men fulfill a role similar to that of
Ulysses' wife, who unwove at night what she had accomplished
during the day. Baltasar's friends have made a similar effort to
control time. For ten years they have collected clocks:

Sentirnos por ello dueños del tiempo o por lo menos del misterio
del tiempo, que es sólo la posibilidad de imaginarlo corriendo hacia

atrás y no hacia adelante el encuentro con el futuro, hasta disolver esa noción y hacerlo todo presente.

(p. 13)

[We . . . feel thus that we own time, or at least the mystery of time, which is to imagine it running backward or speeding us to our meeting with the future, until we reject that idea and define all time as the present.]

(p. 5)

They ultimately fail in their endeavor, although they try to act as if time is not passing while Baltasar is gone. They continue in their earlier jobs, they do not marry, and they are so entirely given to superficial pursuits that they have changed only in outward appearance. Baltasar, in contrast, shows not only signs of physical aging but also an internal maturation. Nonetheless, his Penelope has managed to stop the clock to some degree, as the three friends automatically resume their friendship at the same place where they had paused, ten years prior. Upon Baltasar's urging, Varela and Dorrego leave behind the lifestyle they entertained in his absence, and he is thus reunited with his figurative Penelope. Baltasar is unaware of the fact that there has been an infidelity on Dorrego's part (his affair with Ofelia), but the "couple" is reunited in fraternal bond.

Towards the ending of the novel, Baltasar again sees Gabriela Cóo, the one woman he promised he would love, once he has consummated his love for Ofelia. Although Ofelia never cooperated with Baltasar to fulfill this condition, the novel closes with his newly-rediscovered Gabriela. Thus, the mythic journey of this hero comes to a close. The nations on his continent are free, although their resolve for equality and justice remains to be proven; and his quest for love is probably fulfilled.

The narrator's disclosure of his own affair with Ofelia at the end of the narration accounts for any discrepancies or gaps in the text. Such an admission of subjectivity demands that Varela's account be reread, or at least reconsidered, as a motivated text, like any historical account.

Finally, what remains to complete the hero's journey is for a legendary fame to grow in the land, long after his death, telling of his great feats of bravery. In *La campaña*, this mythic event is replotted to take place in the midst of the heroic journey, which becomes a distracting factor in Baltasar's case. He is fully aware of the heroizing to which he, or a version of himself, is subjected.

After aiding San Martín in a decisive battle and thereby fulfilling his duty as a soldier, Baltasar sets out for Maracaibo in search of Ofelia. On his journey, he encounters the process of his own mythification in the form of the Ballad of Baltasar and Ofelia. His fame precedes him but he becomes uncomfortable with the larger-than-life versions of himself that he hears in every village:

> '¡Vaya héroe!, se dijo Baltasar Bustos, al oír en el hediondo puerto de Buenaventura la primera canción sobre sus amores, convertidos en cumbia y bailados por inmensas negras con pañuelos de cuadros rojos y de cuatro puntas amarradas a la cabeza. . . . ¡Allí viene Baltasar Bustos, buscando a Ofelia Salamanca, de la pampa hasta el llano!'
>
> (p. 172)
>
> [Some hero! Baltasar Bustos said to himself when in the fetid port of Buenaventura he heard the first song about his love, transformed into a *cumbia* and danced . . . by immense black women, their heads decked out in red-checked handkerchiefs tied in fours. . . . Here comes Baltasar Bustos, looking for Ofelia Salamanca, from the pampa to the lowlands!]
>
> (p. 172)

In its many versions, the ballad tells of his great valor and love for Ofelia, and is sung among dancers on the coastline and *criollas* in Panama, spreading quickly, so that his arrival is eagerly awaited in Mexico.

Although he is lauded in the songs, Baltasar rejects the images they portray. He throws away his characteristic wire-rimmed glasses so that he won't be recognized. He is relieved that his military ventures have changed him from the "muchacho de aspecto poco imponente, regordete, melenudo, miope" (p. 172) [a fellow of unimpressive aspect, plump, long-haired, myopic. (p. 172)], to the trim man of tawny, hardened body. Baltasar seems to realize that he is not, in fact, the figure projected in folklore; he is all too conscious of his mortality. For example, although Baltasar is always critical of his rotund physique, he is still tempted by food. Upon hearing the songs in Panama, Baltasar mutters bitterly, "¡Vaya héroe!, que tenía que resistir la tentación de los mantecados y polvorones que se disuelven en la boca." (172) [Some hero—who had to struggle to resist the temptation of shortbread and powder cakes that dissolve on your lips. (p. 172)] Baltasar rejects the hero's image imposed upon him because of his awareness of the discrepancies among the versions of himself in the ballad. This constitutes a postmodern recognition of the constructed, and therefore not inherent or natural, notion of the self; imposing this configuration on Baltasar does not succeed in accurately defining or even denoting his person.

Adding to Baltasar's frustration is the constant reminder that he has not found Ofelia. He wonders if she has heard the songs, and whether she is the cruel woman they depict: "¿Era ella lo que las canciones decían, una amazona a la que le faltaba una teta, cercenada para mejor flechar, hija de un pueblo de puras mujeres que sólo salían a ser preñadas una vez al año y mataban a sus hijos varones?" (p. 175) [Was she what the songs said: an Amazon with one breast cut off, the better to use her bow and arrow, who came from a country exclusively of women, who left it once a year to become pregnant and who killed all male children? (p. 175)] In response to his own question, he muses, "Tampoco era verdad la manera como todas estas baladas lo describían a él." (p. 175) [The way those ballads described him was also not true. (p. 176)] He consequently rejects the ballad's version of Ofelia, who in the songs has quickly become a mysterious, vengeful creature.

The mythic structure of the novel is thereby subverted. Baltasar is a hero who doesn't want to be one, nor is he deluded by the grandeur of becoming a folk hero. The ballads spring up during his lifetime, not after a heroic death, as in classical tales. Baltasar views the ballads only as reminders of his failures and frustration, and takes conscious steps to disassociate himself from them. His journey incorporates mythic conventions, but not as an ordering principle familiar to readers and thus able to contextualize or add significance to the story at hand. Rather, the conventions are exposed and deformed in parodic display. Once it is revealed as a construct, it collapses as an ordering structure and is simply inserted to underscore its useless framework. La campaña becomes a mythic parody, and in the process serves to undermine traditional views of the making of history.

Along with the narrator's problematization of the veracity of his own account, the portrayal of history as myth undercuts the claims by traditional historical texts of their own impartiality. The novel's postmodern treatment of myth also provides a model that admits to being artificially constructed: Baltasar never manages to fill the hero's idealized shoes, and rejects the versions of his person that are narrativized by ballads and imposed upon him. As a near-hero, Fuentes's character demonstrates the scripted nature of the heroic configuration of the self; perhaps the author intends his character to be a metaphor of the artificiality of strictly fashioned and rigidly narrow conceptualizations of the self.

La campaña and *Gringo viejo* thus are postmodern novels that represent the subjectification of history through the exposure of its constructs. They consciously appropriate narrative, mythic, and historical conventions—the hierarchical positioning and chronological sequencing of events, in particular—and disrupt their traditional presentation. The result is a shift in narrative representation of the elements of history, as they are positioned in new, signifying relationships. These texts make no attempt to conceal or to reconcile their often disruptive contradictions. Rather, these historical narratives show the many possible configurations of their altered, nonauthoritative components. In their incorporation of "facts" that are now redefined as constructs, these novels suggest that there exists no single, valid, or natural mode for narration.

However, as Hutcheon notes, "this does not in any way deny the value of history-writing; it merely redefines the condition of value."[8] The underlying dynamic of reading historical accounts is not resolving which version is true, as there are many truths, but seeing the theoretical frameworks guiding each supposition into a position of truth and authority. This involves a plurality of readings, ultimately, as each version contains an implicit positioning of the reader.

In this novel, Carlos Fuentes thus furthers the narrative aims inaugurated definitively, twenty-five years earlier, by *Terra Nostra*. The seven novels to date attempt to inscribe the increasing plurality of a world that Fuentes characterizes as "multipolar and multicultural." Long-held notions of the self, of time, and of the narrative come under forced reconsideration in the reading of his texts. These novels, as expressions of postmodernity, serve as approximations of an unfinished reality.

Conclusion

CARLOS FUENTES SEEKS TO BE REMEMBERED THROUGH THE TELLING, and resuscitated through the reading, of his texts. As records of textual processes, his novels attest to the constructed nature of fiction. In their complexity, they challenge narratives that would repudiate a plural vision of the world.

Fuentes has made public his program of narrative production in an outline entitled "La edad del tiempo."[1] Of the twenty-two works listed by title, some in print and others not yet published, ten novels, short stories and plays were published previous to *Terra Nostra* (1975). As the eleventh and middle text, this novel signals the advent of a new narrative age, in which any authoritative construct—real or textual—becomes suspect.

Fuentes's earlier novels, from *La región más transparente* (1958) to *Cumpleaños* (1969), can best be understood in the light of the Spanish-American Boom period. Challenging rational constructs, the writers of this period experimented with narrative representations of chronology and reality. Many of their characters had exhausted existential questions without finding any answers. *La muerte de Artemio Cruz*, Fuentes's 1962 novel, is considered to be a fundamental text of this period of literature.

In 1982 José Donoso, a Chilean critic and novelist of the Boom, assessed the directions of Spanish-American writers following its two extravagant decades of novelistic production: "Hasn't the time come to sort of turn back a little bit? . . . Can we go on? Of course, one has to arrive at the limit of things to be able to turn back . . . And the whole thing is that we've got to the limit of things."[2] In effect, new writers of the period termed "post-boom" in Spanish America have turned back to simpler narratives (which Donoso terms "modest"). Fuentes, however, has determined a different course of action: turning his back on the notion of an exhausted literary tradition (discussed persuasively in John Barth's essay),[3] he has walked along the precipice of narrative limitation. His post-1970 texts bear witness to the continued vitality of his narrative tradition.

Fuentes, along with his postmodern counterparts world-wide,

is not distressed by the lack of authoritative answers to existential questions. Rather, he accepts the notion of a multiplicity of truths and welcomes the consequent contradictions. The thematics of his novels change as a result; and *Terra Nostra* initiates these transformations.

His narratives written since 1975 no longer identify a self fragmented by his knowledge of the world; instead, they portray the demise of this self as an invariable entity by which to add meaning to life. It is precisely the attempt to guarantee meaning that produces the codification of these elements, which postmodernity holds suspect as artificial constructs.

The notion of time as a chronological and external demarcation of events collapses in texts that consciously undermine its function as an ordering device. Although history is a constant in Fuentes's works, its configurations in the early novels differs significantly from those of recent works. In *La región más transparente*, for instance, the past was an influential presence made visible by Indian characters who subscribed to the circularity of the Aztec concept of time. Characters were urged to remember the past as a means of ensuring a future; the historical was of vital importance to the survival of a nation.

Beginning with Fuentes's eleventh work of fiction, though, the past takes on a much more flexible texture and, complemented by alternate presentations of time, the later novels show the constructed nature of history. Ex-centric versions also shape the past; current reconsiderations alter its present face and influence; this is illustrated particularly in *Gringo viejo* (1985) and *La campaña* (1990). Fuentes's recent narratives depict the past as just as uncertain and variable as the future.

Finally, the postmodern novels of Fuentes hold a nonmimetic view of the textual representation of reality; the transformation of diverse elements of reality forbids this function. This departure from mimesis, however, conveys a more accurate portrayal of his reality. In *Cristóbal Nonato*, the fact that the narrative voice belongs to a fetus and is heard from the womb does not prevent the transmission of a sharply focused view of the plight of Mexico in 1992. Fuentes thus establishes the validity of difference in representation. His own experimentation with narrative conventions—the detective genre in *La cabeza de la hidra* or myth in *La campaña*—attests to the variety of narrative possibilities, which he continues to exploit in all of his novels.

Since the completion of this study, Fuentes has published two additional texts: a collection of novellas entitled *El naranjo, o Los círculos del tiempo* (1993), and the novel, *Diana, o la cazadora solitaria* (1994). It is evident that both texts continue in the course set definitively in *Terra Nostra*.

I mentioned earlier that Fuentes has made public the organizational program of his fiction in "La edad del tiempo." Since 1985, this outline has regularly appeared in each subsequent publication, occasionally with minimal changes (what eventually appears in print as *Diana, o la cazadora solitaria*, for instance, is listed as "Crónica de una actriz renuente"). The outline that appears in *El naranjo*, however, contains an important revision: it adds this title as the final and fourteenth item.

It is significant that the text is subtitled "Los círculos del tiempo." As he draws his narrative plan to a close with a newly final work, Fuentes once again displaces the conclusion of his work in two ways: by adding a title and thereby extending "La edad del tiempo," and by clearly heralding the redoubling upon such a narrative cycle. Indeed, the novellas in this collection— although entirely original—resonate with familiar voices from previous texts within Fuentes's novelistic trajectory. They represent both a reaffirmation and a renewal of familiar themes and of the writer's commitment to formal experimentation.

El naranjo develops themes that both specifically and generally make reference to those present in Fuentes's considerable body of fiction. He examines identity in terms of its relationship to nation and time; the past figures prominently, holding weighty influence over the future; myths (particularly those of Malinche, Colón, Cortés, and Escipión) are revised, rearranged, and otherwise subverted; mirrored figures illustrate the vacuity produced by the excess of endless doubling. Spheres traditionally regarded as separate are superimposed, and traditional boundaries transgressed: life and death are no longer so clearly separate, neither are the self and the other. Additionally, the spatial and temporal coordinates of the five novellas revisit the sites of Carlos Fuentes's previous fictions.

Fuentes elaborates these themes within narratives saturated with continual reminders of the artificial and arbitrary nature of the written word. The self-conscious narrative mode is employed by all narrators in this collection; in "Los hijos del conquistador," the narrative voices of Martín 1 and Martín 2, sons of Cortés, are intercalated as they address each other and the reader. The animosity between them escalates until Martín 1 states:

Me separo de ti, hermano. Te relego de nuevo a la tercera persona, ni siquiera a la segunda que inmerecidamente te vengo dando.

[I'm leaving you, Brother. Once again, I relegate you to the third person, not even to the second in which, without your deserving it, I've been addressing you until now.]⁴

Halved at first, the narrative is further refracted, leaving the reader, always overtly acknowledged, in the midst of a fractured text. Similar images of textual gaps are conveyed in the other novellas by the installation and subversion of binary structures, which multiplies all textual variables. The titles themselves indicate the repetition of this device: "Las dos orillas" [The Two Shores], "Los hijos del conquistador" [Sons of the Conquerer], "Las dos Numancias" [The Two Numantias], "Apolo y las putas" [Apollo and the Whores], and "Las dos Américas" [The Two Americas].

The first novella, "Las dos orillas," is narrated by Jerónimo de Aguilar in sections numbered in reverse order (from ten to one, reminding the reader of Artemio Cruz); he eventually reveals the fact that he is dead, as are the narrators of two other novellas. Like Cristóbal Nonato, who tells us a story from the womb, these narrators transgress constructed boundaries as they address us from the grave.

When Jerónimo asks, "Me pregunto si un evento que no es narrado ocurre en realidad," (p. 58) [I wonder if an event that isn't narrated takes place in reality. (p. 48)] he makes a poignant statement relevant to Fuentes's postmodern fiction. This issue—calling forth questions of mimesis, representation, revisionism, textual variance, and ultimately truth—echoes the questions often posed in Fuentes's fiction, particularly in Una familia lejana—fifteen years prior—and by Varela in La campaña.

Jerónimo's status as a translator, and his particular manipulation of meaning to impose his own desired outcome of events, further problematizes the notion of truth-telling: "Pero cuando palabra, imaginación y mentira se confunden, su producto es la verdad. . . ." (28) [But when words, imagination, and lies jumble together, the result is the truth. . . . (19)] Fuentes's conception of the novel is made plain here, as art adds something to life: the language of the text constructs its own realities.

Nearing the conclusion of his tale, Jerónimo de Aguilar comments on his use of inverted sequence:

Me gusta emplearla hoy, partiendo de diez para llegar a cero, a fin de indicar . . . un perpetuo reinicio de historias perpetuamente inacabadas.

(p. 59)

[I'd like to use it today, beginning with ten and ending with zero, to indicate ... a perpetual rebeginning of stories perpetually unfinished.]

(p. 48)

This narrator thus provides us an apt metaphor for the Mexican writer's guiding novelistic principle: there is no future with a dead past, whether or not it is textually elaborated.

The circularity of the narrative is further developed by the central image of this collection: the orange tree. Reflecting the cycles of fertility, growth, death, and subsequent renewal, the orange tree create a sense of continuity, linking the five sections: images of the tree and its seeds, orange blossoms, and the fruit itself recur in each of the novellas. Jerónimo reports:

Yo planté las semillas de un naranjo que venían, junto con un saco de trigo y una barrica de tinto, en el batel que nos arrojó a estas costas.
(p. 45)
[But I also planted the seeds of an orange tree that came, along with a sack of wheat and a cask of red wine, in the lifeboat that tossed us up on these shores.]
(p. 36)

This tenuous connection—a seed that happens to make its way across the seas—is an appropriate metaphor for the ensuing relationship between Old and New Worlds, to which we are yet witnesses. Origin and future come together in the orange tree; the Iberian Peninsula and the American continent are similarly bound in the cycle, mutually exerting influence and defining their identities.

In the final scene of the last novella, an aged Cristóbal Colón is seated in an airplane, returning to Spain after an unpleasant ejection from Mexico, forced by the tyrannical Señor Nomura: "Oh, cómo gozo viendo desde acá arriba la huella de mi primer viaje, en reversa." (p. 252) [Oh, how I enjoy seeing from up here the trace of my first voyage—in reverse. (p. 228)] Colón never reaches Japan, but Japan comes to him: Mexico has been overtaken by Japanese industry, and Colón has become a disfigured Mamadoc. The apocalyptic portrayal of Mexico's physical and political decadence is clearly reminiscent of earlier works (such as "El que inventó la pólvora," La región más transparente, and Cristóbal Nonato).

Colón holds in one hand the seeds of the orange tree; in the other, he has the key to his house in Toledo. As he recites the

Sephardic prayer he has repeated over the years, he meditates on the following:

> El tiempo circula como las corrientes y todo lo une y relaciona, conquistadores de ayer y de hoy, reconquistas y contraconquistas, paraísos sitiados, apogeos y decadencias, llegadas y partidas, aparici-ones y desapariciones, utopías del recuerdo y del deseo. . . . ¿Qué encontraré al regresar a Europa? Abriré de nuevo la puerta del hogar. Plantaré de nuevo la semilla del naranjo.
>
> (p. 253)
>
> [Time circulates like the currents, uniting and relating everything, yesterday's conquistadors and today's, reconquests and countercon-quests, besieged paradises, pinnacles and decadences, arrivals and departures, appearances and disappearances, utopias of memory and desire. . . . What shall I find when I return to Spain? I shall open the door of my home again. I shall plant the orange seed again.]
>
> (p. 229)

Fuentes thus concludes *El naranjo, o Los círculos del tiempo,* while simultaneously mapping out the patterns of his work: as *El naranjo* closes one narrative cycle, it initiates another. Like the seeds of the orange tree, it points to the beginning of a new and unfinished reality.

In a typically playful rejection of linear chronology, Fuentes publishes a novel one year after the appearance of his "last" work. His 1994 text, *Diana, o la cazadora solitaria,* adopts an autobiographical stance and recounts his affair with Diana Soren, an actress from the United States. The sense of immediacy to the writer is enhanced by the specificity of events in the U.S. that were featured in news coverage during 1992 (the Midwest-ern floods and Michael Jackson), and in general to the icons of popular culture from the sixties and the seventies.

The novel's mythic overtones provide a superstructure that lends itself to postmodern subversion: Diana is seeking an ideal of love, identity, and justice; and yet her moonlit hunting comes to naught. The cinematographic allusions are also fertile playing fields for the notions of artificiality, construct, and framing, which are successfully exploited in this postmodern novel.

This is a novel that denies readers the opportunity to lose themselves in the reading, to forget for a moment that there is a subjective ordering of events, executed at the whim of a writer. There are constant second-person "intrusions," signaling an ir-revocable, postmodern narrative presence. The reader is re-minded repeatedly of the essence of the text as a mediated entity:

Esta narración lastrada por las pasiones del tiempo se derrota a sí misma porque jamás alcanzará la perfección ideal de lo que se puede imaginar.

[This narrative, weighed down by the passions of time, defeats itself, because it will never achieve the ideal perfection of what can be imagined. (p. 9)][5]

The world created in this text is always only this: a verbal construct, product of memory and telling, existing only through words that are read by a different reader, "La novela no debe ser leída como fue escrita." (p. 12) [The novel should not be read as it was written (p. 6)] He adds, "Esta condición se vuelve extremadamente azarosa en una crónica autobiográfica." (p. 12) [This condition becomes extremely dangerous in an autobiographical text (p. 6)] Thus, not only is the variance of reading embedded in the text, but the plurality of writing becomes an acknowledged norm of fiction.

Near the end of this novel, the narrator assesses his experience as a writer, that might well be extended to the postmodern writer generally:

Con esa novela encontré a mis verdaderos lectores, los que quería crear, descubrir, tener. Los que, conmigo, querían encontrar la figura de una máxima inseguridad constitutiva, no sicologías agotadas, sino figuras desvalidas, gestándose en otro rango de la comunicación y el discurso: la lengua, la historia, las épocas, las ausencias, las inexistencias como personajes, y la novela como el lugar de encuentro de tiempos y seres que de otra manera, jamás se darán la mano.

(p. 209)

[With that novel, I found my real readers, those whom I wanted to create, discover, keep. Those who, like me, wanted to discover the figure of greatest essential insecurity—not worn-out psychologies but helpless figures developing at another level of communication and discourse: language, history, epochs, absences, non-existences as characters, and the novel as the meeting place of times and beings that would never otherwise encounter one another.

(p. 196)]

Fuentes alludes to the paradigm that has defined the contours of his fiction: the novel as creator of a plane of existence all its own, independent from extratextual reality; the novel as process; the novel as facilitator of encounters of disparate elements—the Quijote, after all, is at least as real to us as Miguel de Cervantes— these things point to the text as postmodern writers would like it to be seen.

In the same year that *El naranjo* appeared in print, Fuentes published a series of critical essays that addresses the question, "Has the novel died?"[6] His comments—regarding works of individuals whose names would indubitably appear on lists of "Postmodern Writers"—can be considered a manifesto of narrative independence and an impassioned endorsement of the continued vitality and originality of the novel. Perhaps his thoughts are best summed up in the following comment: "La novela es una búsqueda verbal de lo que espera ser escrito." (p. 36) [The novel is a verbal search for what waits to be written.]

Carlos Fuentes is undoubtedly one of the most significant Spanish-American writers, whose contribution gives continued evidence of important points of convergence with writers worldwide. Like other postmodern writers, he engages a plural view of the world; his is an active dialogue, of speaking perceptively and listening eloquently. Certainly an impressive legacy stands behind him, awaiting future readings; just as surely, contiguous realities wait to be written.

Notes

All translations throughout the book are mine unless otherwise noted.

INTRODUCTION

1. See William H. Gass, "The First Seven Pages of the Boom," *Latin American Literary Review* 15, no. 29 (1987), 33–56; John King, editor, *On Modern Latin American Fiction* (New York: Farrar, Straus and Giroux, 1987); Donald Shaw, "Which Was the First Novel of the Boom?" *Modern Language Review* 89, no.2 (1994), 360–71 and his *Nueva narrativa hispanoamericana* (Madrid: Cátedra, 1985); Philip Swanson, editor, *Landmarks in Modern Latin American Fiction* (London: Routledge, 1990).

2. Donald Shaw, "The First Novel of the Boom," p. 364.

3. Roberto González Echevarría, "Sarduy, the Boom, and the Post-Boom," *Latin American Literary Review* 15, no. 29 (1987), 61.

4. John S. Brushwood, "Two Views of the Boom: North and South," *Latin American Literary Review* 15, no. 29 (1987), 13–31.

5. It is interesting to note that Jorge Luis Borges's *Ficciones* (1944) is often regarded—as is the case with Vladimir Nabokov—to be a clear precursor to contemporary postmodern textual expression. In typical postmodern fashion, textual configurations often predate critical awareness of their form.

CHAPTER 1. APPROACHING POSTMODERNISM: FROM *LA REGIÓN MÁS TRANSPARENTE* (1958) TO *TERRA NOSTRA* (1975)

1. Carlos Fuentes, "The Power of the Written Word," Elizabethtown College (Pennsylvania), September 27, 1990. Early forerunners to some of the postulations made in the lecture appear in Fuentes's essay, *La nueva novela hispanoamericana* (México: Mortiz, 1967) and in his interview with Debra A. Castillo entitled "Travails with Time: An Interview with Carlos Fuentes," *Review of Contemporary Fiction* 8, no. 2 (1988): 153–65.

2. Ibid.

3. Linda Hutcheon, *A Poetics of Postmodernism* (London: Routledge, 1988), ix.

4. See for example Ihab Hassan, *The Postmodern Turn: Essays in Postmodern Theory and Culture* (Columbus: Ohio State University Press, 1987), 91. The author presents a chart with modernist characteristics in one column and postmodernist ones in another, thus limiting their relationship to a binary opposition.

5. John Barth, "Postmodernism Revisited," *The Review of Contemporary Fiction* 8, no. 2 (1988), 16.

6. Brian McHale, *Postmodernist Fiction* (New York: Methuen, 1987).

7. Fuentes, "The Power of the Written Word."

8. Edward Mendelson, "*Gravity's Rainbow*" in *Mindful Pleasures*, edited by George Levine and David Leverenz (Boston: Little, Brown, 1976), 163.

9. In response to my question regarding characterization in one of his novels, Carlos Fuentes explained that the best term for his characters is "figures," as it more accurately denotes their indeterminacy of form.

10. Fuentes has stated in an interview that, "No me agrada repetir lo que ya sé hacer, sino indagar lo que no puedo hacer." Emir Rodríguez Monegal, "Carlos Fuentes" in *Homenaje a Carlos Fuentes: Variaciones en torno a su obra*, edited by Helmy F. Giacoman (New York: Las Américas, 1971), 48.

11. Lanin Gyurko, "*La muerte de Artemio Cruz* and *Citizen Kane*: A Comparative Analysis," in *Carlos Fuentes: A Critical View*, edited by Robert Brody and Charles Rossman (Austin: University of Texas Press, 1982), 64–69.

12. Jonathan Tittler, "*Cambio de piel/Zona sagrada*: Transfiguration in Carlos Fuentes," *World Literature Today* 57, no. 4 (1983), 537.

13. Wendy Faris, *Carlos Fuentes* (New York: Ungar, 1983), 23.

14. Carlos Fuentes, *Zona sagrada* (Mexico: Siglo XXI Editores, 1967), 65; and Carlos Fuentes, *Holy Place*, translated by Suzanne Jill Levine in *Triple Cross* (New York: E.F. Dutton, 1972), 55.

15. Gloria Durán, *The Archetypes of Carlos Fuentes: From Witch to Androgyne* (Hambden, CT: The Shoe String Press), 95.

16. Ibid., 97.

17. Emir Rodríguez Monegal, "Carlos Fuentes," in *Homenaje a Carlos Fuentes*, edited by Helmy F. Giacoman (New York: Las Américas, 1971), 116.

18. Robert A. Parsons, "The 'Vision of Horror' or 'Opposing Self': The Double in Three Novels by Carlos Fuentes." *Journal of Evolutionary Psychology* 8 (1987), 107.

19. Shirley A. Williams, "The Quest for Quetzalcoatl and Total Fiction," *Hispanic Journal* 8, no. 1 (Fall 1986), 121.

20. Bernard Fouques, "Escritura y diferencia: *Cambio de piel* de Carlos Fuentes," *Cuadernos Americanos* 44, no. 5 (1985), 224.

21. Rodríguez Monegal, 63.

22. Ferndando F. Salcedo, "Los 'monjes': Personajes claves en *Cambio de piel* de Carlos Fuentes," *Hispanófila* 25, no. 75 (1982), 78.

23. Ibid., 78.

24. See note 9, above.

25. Margaret Sayers Peden, "*Terra Nostra*: Fact and Fiction," *The American Hispanist* 1, no. 1 (1975), 5.

26. ibid., 6.

27. Carlos Fuentes, *Terra Nostra* (Barcelona: Seix Barral, 1975), 397; and Carlos Fuentes, *Terra Nostra*, translated by Margaret Sayers Peden (New York: Farrar, Straus and Giroux, 1976), 391.

28. Walter Reed, *An Exemplary History of the Novel* (Chicago: University of Chicago Press, 1981), 280.

29. Nicolás Toscano traces the sources for Fuentes' incorporation of paintings in the novel, showing the influence of Colonial, Baroque, and Renaissance art. See his article, "*Terra Nostra* y la pintura," *Cuadernos Americanos* 4

(1990), 196 and 198, for a complete discussion of the subversion in Bosch and Signorelli's paintings, as re-created by Fuentes in his text. The author himself has commented on the significance of the innovations of Signorelli's art in his essay, *Cervantes o la crítica de la lectura* (Mexico: Mortiz, 1976), 4. Fuentes states, "Las formas y los espacios de Signorelli giran, fluyen, se transforman, se dilatan."

30. Evelia Cavalheiro, "The Iconic Text as Pre-Text and Pretext in Carlos Fuentes' *Terra Nostra*," in *Interpretaciones a la obra de Carlos Fuentes*, edited by Ana María Hernández de López (Madrid: Beramar, 1990), 179.

31. Lanin Gyurko, "Novel Into Essay: Fuentes' *Terra Nostra* as Generator of *Cervantes o la crítica*," *Mester* 11, 2 (1983), 22.

32. See, in addition to Gyurko's essay in note 31, the following articles: Catherine Swietlicki, "Doubling, Reincarnation, and Comic Order in *Terra Nostra*," *Hispanófila* 27, no. 1 (1983): 93–104; Susan F. Levine, "The Lesson of the *Quijote* in the Works of Carlos Fuentes and Juan Goytisolo," *Journal of Spanish Studies: Twentieth Century* 7 (1979), 173–85; and Raymond L. Williams, "Observaciones sobre el doble en *Terra Nostra*," in *Simposio Carlos Fuentes: Actas*, edited by Juan Loveluck and Isaac Levy (Univ. of South Carolina: 1980), 175–83.

33. Joel D. Black, "Paper Empires of the New World: Pynchon, Gaddis, Fuentes," in *Proceedings of Xth Congress of the International Comparative Literature Association*, III (New York: Garland, 1985), 74.

CHAPTER 2. REFLECTIONS OF A NARRATOR: *UNA FAMILIA LEJANA* (1980)

1. For an elaboration of the nature of the demonic in the novel, see Lanin Gyurko's "The Self and the Demonic in Fuentes' *Una familia lejana*," *Revista/Review Iberoamericana* 12 (1982/83), 572–620.

2. Carlos Fuentes, *Una familia lejana* (Mexico: Ediciones Era, 1980), 169; and Carlos Fuentes, *Distant Relations*, translated by Margaret Sayers Peden (New York: Farrar, Straus and Giroux, 1982) 176.

3. Roland Barthes. *Image/Music/Text*, translated by Stephen Heath (New York: Hill and Wang, 1977), 157.

4. Fernando Burgos, "Visiones íntimas de *Una familia lejana*," *Inti* 28 (1988), 4.

5. Margaret Sayers Peden, "Forking Paths, Infinite Novels, Ultimate Narrators," in *Carlos Fuentes: A Critical View*, edited by Robert Brody and Charles Rossman (Austin: University of Texas Press, 1982), 160.

6. John Barth, "The Literature of Exhaustion," *Atlantic Monthly* 220 (1967): 29–34.

7. Incidentally, Barth responds similarly in his 1988 essay, "The Literature of Replenishment: Postmodernist Fiction," *Atlantic Monthly* 245 (1980), 65–71.

8. John Hawkes, *Travesty*, 5th ed. (New York: New Directions, 1976), 102.

9. Martha Paley Francescato attributes this statement to Fuentes in "*Distant Relations*: Chronicle of Various Close Readings," *World Literature Today* 57 (1983), 594.

10. See the special issue on Fuentes in *Quimera: Revista de Crítica Literaria* 68 (1987), 63.

CHAPTER 3. CRISES OF IDENTITY: TEXT AND THE SELF IN *LA CABEZA DE LA HIDRA* (1978)

1. Lanin Gyurko, "Self and the Double in Fuentes' *La cabeza de la hidra*," *Ibero-Amerikanisches Archiv* 7, no. 3 (1981), 240.

2. Lanin Gyurko has conducted an essential study of doubling at all levels in the novel in "Self and Double in Fuentes' *La cabeza de la hidra*" (see note 1). He further explores the implications for Mexico's state of affairs in "Individual and National Identity in Fuentes's *La cabeza de la hidra*," in *Latin American Fiction Today*, edited by Rose S. Minc (Upper Montclair, New Jersey: Hispamérica, 1979), 33–47.

3. Philip Koldewyn, "*La cabeza de la hidra*: Residuos del colonialismo," *Mester* 11, no. 1 (1982), 51.

4. Gyurko, "Individual and National Identity," 36.

5. Carlos Fuentes, *La cabeza de la hidra* (Barcelona: Argos, 1978), 132; and Carlos Fuentes, *The Hydra Head*, translated by Margaret Sayers Peden (New York: Farrar, Straus and Giroux, 1978), 135.

6. For a discussion of the doubling of Félix and Velázquez, see Mary E. Davis's two excellent studies: "The Twins in the Looking Glass: Carlos Fuentes' *La cabeza de la hidra*," *Hispania* 65 (1982), 371–76; and "On Becoming Velázquez: Carlos Fuentes' *The Hydra Head*," in *Carlos Fuentes: A Critical View*, edited by Robert Brody and Charles Rossman (Austin: University of Texas Press, 1982), 146–55.

7. Although most critics make reference to the cinematic intertextuality of *La cabeza de la hidra*, McNerney and Martin's study is the most specific to date. See their article, "Not a One-Way Street: Film to Novel in *La cabeza de la hidra*," in *Interpretaciones a la obra de Carlos Fuentes*, edited by Ana María Hernández de López (Madrid: Beramar, 1990), 183–88.

8. Gyurko, "Individual and National Identity," 44.

9. Ibid., 45.

10. Gyurko, "Self and the Double," 247.

11. Ibid., 244.

12. Ibid., 244.

13. See note 6.

CHAPTER 4. ISSUES OF NATIONAL AND NARRATIVE CONTROL: *CRISTÓBAL NONATO* (1987)

1. Carlos Fuentes, *Cristóbal Nonato* (Mexico: Fondo de Cultura Económica, 1987), 85; and Carlos Fuentes, *Christopher Unborn*, translated by Alfred Mac Adam and Carlos Fuentes (New York: Farrar, Straus and Giroux, 1989), 76.

2. The misuse of Spanish punctuation—the text omits inverted question marks, and is inconsistent in that it uses inverted exclamation marks—is another instance of the loss of Mexican commonality and autonomy at the hands of massive Anglicization.

3. Maarten van Delden, "The View from the Womb," Review of *Cristóbal Nonato*, by Carlos Fuentes, *New Leader*, 27 November, 1989, 18.

4. Leticia Reyes-Tatinclaux, "*Cristóbal nonato*, ¿descubrimiento o clausura del Nuevo Mundo?" *Revista de Crítica Literaria Latinoamericana* 15, no. 30 (1989), 102.

5. The English translation of this passage falls short of its Spanish counterpart, as it completely loses its sonorous element; and it is clear why this is one of several sections omitted from the English translation of the novel.

6. Julio Ortega, "Christopher Unborn: Rage and Laughter." *Review of Contemporary Fiction* 8, no. 2 (1988), 287.

7. "Don't try to evaporate on me," p. 103; and "All together now," p. 148. As explained above (see note 5), certain word plays are simply lost in translation.

8. This fragment is impossible to translate; indeed, it was omitted from the author's translation.

9. Ironically, the winner of the 1991 Miss Universe Pageant was a Mexican named Lupita Jones.

10. For a complete discussion of Fuentes' theory of reading, see his essay, *Cervantes o la crítica de la lectura* (Mexico: Joaquín Mortiz, 1976).

11. Jean Baudrillard, *Simulations*. translated by Paul Foss, Paul Patton, and Philip Beitchman (New York: Semiotext(e), 1983), 3.

CHAPTER 5. RECONSIDERATIONS OF THE PAST: *GRINGO VIEJO* (1985) AND *LA CAMPAÑA* (1990)

1. Although a significant faction of postmodern theorists, led by Fredric Jameson, contends that postmodernity is ahistorical, an equally respected group, led by Linda Hutcheon, refutes this view. Representative postmodern authors situate their narratives within historical contexts and engage the past and present in a critical confrontation. In addition, the different versions of the past do not nullify the concept of history; rather, they underscore its vitality and continuing influence on the present.

2. See Hutcheon's comprehensive study, *A Poetics of Postmodernism* (New York: Routledge, 1988), particularly Part II, pp 105–231.

3. Ibid., 97.

4. Ibid., 114.

5. Carlos Fuentes, *Gringo viejo* (Mexico: Fondo de Cultura Económica, 1985), 61; and Carlos Fuentes, *The Old Gringo*, translated by Margaret Sayers Peden and Carlos Fuentes (New York: Farrar, Straus and Giroux, 1985), 58.

6. See Joseph Chrzanowski, "Patricide and the Double in Carlos Fuentes' *Gringo viejo*," *The International Fiction Review* 16, no. 1 (1989), 11–16; see also Joaquín Roy, "Historia, biografía, cine y ficción," *Revista de Crítica Literaria Latinoamericana* 15, 30 (1989), 99–104.

7. Carlos Fuentes, *La campaña* (Madrid: Mondadori, 1990), 211; and Carlos Fuentes, *The Campaign*, translated by Alfred Mac Adam (New York: Farrar, Straus and Giroux, 1991), 215.

8. Hutcheon, 129.

CONCLUSION

1. The outline first appears in the edition of *Gringo viejo* published by the Fondo de Cultura Económica, 1985.

2. Cited by Ronald Christ in "An Interview with José Donoso." *Parisian Review* 49 (1982), 23–44.

3. See John Barth's essay, "The Literature of Exhaustion," *Atlantic Monthly* 220 (August 1967), 29–34.

4. Carlos Fuentes, *El naranjo, o Los círculos del tiempo* (Mexico: Alfaguara, 1993), 78; and Carlos Fuentes, *The Orange Tree,* translated by Alfred Mac Adam (New York: Farrar, Straus and Giroux, 1994), 65.

5. Carlos Fuentes, *Diana o la cazadora solitaria* (Mexico: Alfaguara, 1994), 15; and Carlos Fuentes, *Diana, the Goddess Who Hunts Alone,* translated by Alfred Mac Adam (New York: Farrar, Straus and Giroux, 1995), 9.

6. Carlos Fuentes, *Geografía de la novela* (Mexico: Alfaguara, 1993).

Bibliography

Alazraki, Jaime and David Draper Clark. "*Terra Nostra*: Coming to Grips With History." *World Literature Today* 57, no. 4 (1983): 551–58.

Alonso, Carlos J. "The Mourning After: García Márquez, Fuentes, and the Meaning of Postmodernity in Spanish America." *Modern Language Notes* 109 (1994): 252–67.

Barth, John. "The Literature of Exhaustion." *Atlantic Monthly* 220 (1967): 29–34.

———. "The Literature of Replenishment: Postmodernist Fiction." *Atlantic Monthly* 245 (1980): 65–71.

———. *Once Upon a Time.* Boston: Little, Brown and Company, 1994.

———. "Postmodernism Revisited." *The Review of Contemporary Fiction* 8, no. 2 (1988): 16–24.

Barthes, Roland. *Image/Music/Text.* Translated by Stephen Heath. New York: Hill and Wang, 1977.

Baudrillard, Jean. *Simulations.* Translated by Paul Foss, Paul Patton, and Philip Beitchman. New York: Semiotext(e), 1983.

Beverly, John. "Postmodernism in Latin America." *Siglo XX* 9, no. 1–2 (1991–92): 9–30.

Black, Joel D. "Paper Empires of the New World: Pynchon, Gaddis, Fuentes." In *Proceedings of Xth Congress of the International Comparative Literature Association.* Vol. 3. New York: Garland, 1985.

Boldy, Steven. "*Cambio de piel*: Literature and Evil." *Bulletin of Hispanic Studies* 66 (1989): 55–72.

———. "Intertextuality in Carlos Fuentes's *Gringo viejo*." *Romance Quarterly* 39, no. 4 (1992): 489–500.

Boling, Becky. "*Terra Nostra*: desmitificación de la historia." *Cuadernos Americanos* 4 (1990): 200–16.

Booker, Keith M. *Vargas Llosa Among the Postmodernists.* Gainesville: University Press of Florida, 1994.

Brody, Robert and Charles Rossman. *Carlos Fuentes: A Critical View.* Austin: University of Texas Press, 1982.

Brushwood, John S. "Sobre el referente y la transformación narrativa en las novelas de Carlos Fuentes y Gustavo Sainz." *Revista Iberoamericana* 47, no. 116–17 (1981): 49–54.

———. "Two Views of the Boom: North and South." *Latin American Literary Review* 15, no. 29 (1987): 13–31.

Burgos, Fernando. "Visiones íntimas de *Una familia lejana*." *Inti* 28 (1988): 3–14.

Castillo, Debra A. "Fantastic Arabesques in Fuentes' *Cristóbal Nonato*." *Revista de Estudios Hispánicos* 25, no. 3 (1991): 1–14.

———. "Tongue in the Ear: Fuentes' *Gringo viejo*." *Revista Canadiense de Estudios Hispánicos* 14, no. 1 (1989): 35–49.

———. "Travails with Time: An Interview with Carlos Fuentes." *Review of Contemporary Fiction* 8, no. 2 (1988): 153–65.

Cavalherio, Evelia. "The Iconic Text as Pre-Text and Pretext in Carlos Fuentes' *Terra Nostra*." In *Interpretaciones a la obra de Carlos Fuentes*. Edited by Ana María Hernández de López. Madrid: Beramar, 1990.

Christ, Ronald. "An Interview with José Donoso. "*Parisian Review* 49 (1982): 23–44.

Chrzanowski, Joseph. "Patricide and the Double in Carlos Fuentes' *Gringo viejo*." *The International Fiction Review* 16, no. 1 (1989): 11–16.

Colás, Santiago. "Translating Postmodernism." In *Translating Latin America: Culture as Text, Translation Perspectives VI*, edited by William Luis and Julio Rodríguez-Luis. Binghampton: SUNY Press, 1991.

Coover, Robert and Dolors Udina. "Un círculo gigantesco." *Quimera* 68 (1987): 44–47.

Davis, Mary E. "The Haunted Voice: Echoes of William Faulkner in García Márquez, Fuentes, and Vargas Llosa." *World Literature Today* 59 (1985): 531–35.

———. "On Becoming Velázquez: Carlos Fuentes' *The Hydra Head*. In *Carlos Fuentes: A Critical View*, edited by Robert Brody and Charles Rossman. Austin: University of Texas Press, 1982.

———. "The Twins in the Looking Glass: Carlos Fuentes' *La cabeza de la hidra*." *Hispania* 65 (1982): 371–76.

Davenport, Guy. "*Distant Relations*: A Conjunction of Opposites." *Review of Contemporary Fiction* 8, no. 2 (1988): 234–37.

De Valdés, María Elena. "La trinidad femenina en *Gringo viejo* de Carlos Fuentes." *Revista Canadiense de Estudios Hispánicos* 14, no. 3 (1990): 415–30.

———. "Fuentes on Mexican Feminophobia." *The Review of Contemporary Fiction* 8, no. 2 (1988): 225–33.

D'haen, Theo and Hans Bertens, eds. *Postmodernist Fiction in Europe and the Americas*. Amsterdam: Rodopi, 1988.

Downing, David B. and Susan Bazargan, eds. *Image and Ideology in Modern/ Postmodern Discourse*. Albany, NY: Suny Press, 1991.

Durán, Gloria. *The Archetypes of Carlos Fuentes: From Witch to Androgyne*. Hambden, CT: The Shoe String Press, 1980.

———. "*Terra Nostra* or 'It Seems to Me I've Heard that Song Before.'" *The American Hispanist* 3, no. 24 (1978): 4–7.

Durán, Manuel. *Tríptico mexicano: Juan Rulfo, Carlos Fuentes, Salvador Elizondo*. Mexico: Secretaría de Educación Pública, 1973.

Echegoyen, Regina N. "La función intertextual de las crónicas en *Terra Nostra*." *Cuadernos Americanos* 6, no. 3 (1992): 108–14.

Echevarren, Roberto. "La literariedad: *Respiración artificial*, de Ricardo Piglia." *Revista Iberoamericana* 49, no. 125 (1983): 997–1008.

Faris, Wendy B. *Carlos Fuentes*. New York: Frederick Ungar Publishing Co., 1983.

———. "Desire and Power, Love and Revolution: Carlos Fuentes and Milan Kundera. *Review of Contemporary Fiction* 8, no. 2 (1988): 273–84.

Foster, Hal, ed. *The Anti-Aesthetic: Essays on Postmodern Culture*. Port Townsend, WA: Bay Press, 1983.

Fouques, Bernard. "Escritura y diferencia: *Cambio de piel* de Carlos Fuentes." *Cuadernos Americanos* 44, no. 5 (1985): 223–31.

Freeman, Christine. "Speaking the Silent Mutiny of the Muted: Narrative Heresy in Fuentes' *Terra Nostra* and Pynchon's *Gravity's Rainbow*." Ph.D. diss., Kent State University, 1984. Abstract in *Dissertation Abstracts International* 45 (1984): 3127A.

Fuentes, Carlos. *Agua quemada*. Mexico: Fondo de Cultura Económica, 1981.

———. *Aura*. Mexico: Ediciones Era, 1962.

———. *Aura*. Translated by Lysander Kemp. Bilingual Edition. New York: Farrar, Straus and Giroux, 1968.

———. *Las buenas conciencias*. Mexico: Fondo de Cultura Económica, 1959.

———. *Burnt water*. Translated by Margaret Sayers Peden. New York: Farrar, Straus and Giroux, 1980.

———. *La cabeza de la hidra*. Barcelona: Argos, 1978.

———. *Cambio de piel*. Mexico: Joaquín Mortiz, 1964.

———. *The Campaign*. Translated by Alfred Mac Adam. New York: Farrar, Straus and Giroux, 1991.

———. *La campaña*. Madrid: Mondadori, 1990.

———. *Cantar de ciegos*. Mexico: Joaquín Mortiz, 1964.

———. *Casa con dos puertas*. Mexico: Joaquín Mortiz, 1970.

———. *Cervantes o la crítica de la lectura*. Mexico: Joaquín Mortiz, 1976.

———. *A Change of Skin*. Translated by Sam Hileman. New York: Farrar, Straus and Giroux, 1968.

———. *Christopher Unborn*. Translated by Alfred Mac Adam and Carlos Fuentes. New York: Farrar, Straus and Giroux, 1989.

———. *Constancia and Other Stories for Virgins*. Translated by Thomas Christensen. New York: Farrar, Straus and Giroux, 1990.

———. *Constancia y otros cuentos para vírgines*. Mexico: Fondo de Cultura Económica, 1988.

———. *Cristóbal Nonato*. Mexico: Fondo de Cultura Económica, 1987.

———. *Cumpleaños*. Mexico: Joaquín Mortiz, 1969.

———. *The Death of Artemio Cruz*. Translated by Alfred Mac Adam. New York: Farrar, Straus and Giroux, 1991.

———. *Diana, the Goddess Who Hunts Alone*. Translated by Alfred Mac Adam. New York: Farrar, Straus and Giroux, 1995.

———. *Diana o la cazadora solitaria*. Mexico: Alfaguara, 1994.

———. *Distant Relations*. Translated by Margaret Sayers Peden. New York: Farrar, Straus and Giroux, 1982.

———. *Los días enmascarados*. Mexico: Los Presentes, 1954.

———. *Una familia lejana*. Mexico: Ediciones Era, 1980.

———. *Gabriel García Márquez and the Invention of America*. Liverpool: Liverpool University Press, 1987.

———. *Geografía de la novela*. Mexico: Alfaguara, 1993.

———. *The Good Conscience.* Translated by Sam Hileman. New York: Ivan Obolensky, 1964.

———. *Gringo viejo.* Mexico: Fondo de Cultura Económica, 1985.

———. *Holy Place.* Translated by Suzanne Jill Levine in *Triple Cross.* New York: E.F. Dutton, 1972.

———. *The Hydra Head.* Translated by Margaret Sayers Peden. New York: Farrar, Straus and Giroux, 1978.

———. *La muerte de Artemio Cruz.* Mexico: Fondo de Cultura Económica, 1962.

———. *El mundo de José Luis Cuevas.* Bilingual Edition, translated by Consuelo de Aerenlund. Mexico: Galería de Arte Misrachi, 1969.

———. *Myself With Others.* New York: Farrar, Straus and Giroux, 1988.

———. *El naranjo, o Los círculos del tiempo.* Mexico: Alfaguara, 1993.

———. *La nueva novela hispanoamericana.* Mexico: Joaquín Mortiz, 1969.

———. *The Old Gringo.* Translated by Margaret Sayers Peden and Carlos Fuentes. New York: Farrar, Straus and Giroux, 1985.

———. *The Orange Tree.* Translated by Alfred Mac Adam. New York: Farrar, Straus and Giroux, 1994.

———. *Orguídeas a la luz de la luna.* Barcelona: Seix Barral, 1982.

———. *París, la revolución de Mayo.* Mexico: Ediciones Era, 1968.

———. *La región más transparente.* Mexico: Fondo de Cultura Económica, 1958.

———. *Los reinos originarios.* Barcelona: Barral Editores, 1971.

———. *Righe per Adami.* Venice: Alpieri, 1968.

———. *Terra Nostra.* Barcelona: Seix Barral, 1975.

———. *Terra Nostra.* Translated by Margaret Sayers Peden. New York: Farrar, Straus and Giroux, 1976.

———. *Tiempo mexicano.* Mexico: Joaquín Mortiz, 1970.

———. *Todos los gatos son pardos.* Mexico: Siglo XXI Editores, 1970.

———. *Valiente nuevo mundo.* Madrid: Mondadori, 1990.

———. *Where the Air is Clear.* Translated by Sam Hileman. New York: Ivan Obolensky, 1960.

———. *Zona sagrada.* Mexico: Siglo XXI Editores, 1967.

García Gutiérrez, Georgina. "*Cristóbal Nonato*: Profecía apocalíptica, experimentación lúdica, crítica certera." *Cuadernos Americanos* 4 (1990): 167–90.

García Núñez, Fernando. "La frontera norte de México en *Gringo viejo* de Carlos Fuentes." *Plural* 17, no. 6 (1988): 41–44.

———. "La imposibilidad del libre albedrío en *La cabeza dela hidra* de Carlos Fuentes." *Cuadernos Americanos* 43, no. 1 (1984): 227–34.

Gass, William H. "The First Seven Pages of the Boom." *Latin American Literary Review* 15, no. 29 (1987): 35–56.

Garza-Cuaron, Beatriz. "Nonatos literarios. Búsqueda del origen y gestación de la conciencia." *Estudios de Folklore y literatura dedicados a Mercedes Díaz Roig.* México: Colegio de México, 1992.

Giacoman, Helmy F., ed. *Homenaje a Carlos Fuentes: Variaciones en torno a su obra.* New York: Las Américas, 1971.

González, Alfonso. "Krause's 'Carlos Fuentes: Toward the Creation of a Myth.'" *International Fiction Review* 16, no. 2 (1989): 98–102.

González, Ann Brashear. "'La novela totalizadora': Pynchon's *Gravity's Rainbow* and Fuentes' *Terra Nostra*." Ph.D. diss., Rutgers University, 1984. Abstract in *Dissertation Abstracts International* 44 (1984): 3057A–58A.

González Echevarría, Roberto. "Sarduy, the Boom, and the Post-Boom." *Latin American Literary Review* 15, no. 29 (1987): 57–72.

Goytisolo, Juan. "*Terra Nostra*." *Review* 19 (1976): 4–24.

Gretel, Zunilda. "Semiótica, historia y ficción en *Terra Nostra*." *Revista Iberoamericana* 47, no. 116–17 (1981): 63–72.

Gutiérrez, Carl. "Provisional Historicity: Reading Through *Terra Nostra*." *Review of Contemporary Fiction* 8, no. 2 (1988): 257–65.

Gyurko, Lanin A. "Individual and National Identity in Fuentes' *La cabeza de la hidra*." In *Latin American Fiction Today*, edited by Rose S. Minc. Upper Montclair, New Jersey: Hispamérica, 1979.

———. "*La muerte de Artemio Cruz* and *Citizen Kane*: A Comparative Analysis." In *Carlos Fuentes: A Critical View*, edited by Robert Brody and Charles Rossman. Austin: University of Texas Press, 1982.

———. "Novel Into Essay: Fuentes' *Terra Nostra* as Generator of *Cervantes o la crítica*." *Mester* 11, no. 2 (1983): 16–35.

———. "The Self and the Demonic in Fuentes' *Una familia lejana*." *Revista/ Review Iberoamericana* 12 (1982/83): 572–620.

———. "Self and the Double in Fuentes' *La cabeza de la hidra*." *Ibero-Amerikanisches Archiv* 7, no. 3 (1981): 239–63.

Hardy, Karen. "Freddy Lambert as 'Narractor' of *Cambio de piel*." *Hispania* 6 (1978): 270–78.

Hassan, Ihan. *The Postmodern Turn: Essays in Postmodern Theory and Culture*. Columbus: Ohio State University Press, 1987.

Hawkes, John. *Travesty*, 5th ed. New York: New Directions, 1976.

Hernández de López, Ana María, ed. *Interpretaciones a la obra de Carlos Fuentes*. Madrid: Beramar, 1990.

———, ed. *La obra de Carlos Fuentes: Una visión múltiple*. Madrid: Pliegos, 1988.

Holt, Candace K. "*Terra Nostra*: Indagación de una identidad." *Revista de estudios hispánicos* 17, no. 3 (1983): 395–406.

Hutcheon, Linda. *A Poetics of Postmodernism*. New York: Routledge, 1988.

———. *The Politics of Postmodernism*. New York: Routledge, 1989.

Huyssen, Andreas. *After the Great Divide*. Bloomington: Indiana University Press, 1986.

Jameson, Fredric. *Postmodernism, or, The Cultural Logic of Late Capitalism*. Durham: Duke University Press, 1991.

Jiménez, Marilyn. "The Incarcerated Narrator: A Study of the Narrative Situation in Samuel Beckett's *Watt* and Carlos Fuentes' *Cambio de piel*." Ph.D. diss, Columbia University, 1981.

Josephs, Allen. "The End of *Terra Nostra*." *World Literature Today* 57, no. 4 (1983): 564–67.

Juan-Santiago, Navarro. "En busca de la utopía: La novela como alegoría de la nación en *Cristóbal Nonato* de Carlos Fuentes." *Explicación de Textos Literarios* 20, no. 1 (1991–92): 24–46.

Jung, C. G. *Man and His Symbols*. New York: Bantam, 1968.

Kadir, Djelal. "Carlos Fuentes: Culpable inocencia y profeta del pasado." *Revista Iberoamericana* 47, no. 116–17 (1981): 55–61.

Kennedy, William. "Carlos Fuentes: Dreaming of History." *Review of Contemporary Fiction* 8, no. 2 (1988): 234–37.

King, John, ed. *On Modern Latin American Fiction*. New York: Farrar, Straus and Giroux, 1987.

Koldewyn, Philip. "*La cabeza de la hidra*: Residuos del colonialismo," *Mester* 11, no. 1 (1982): 47–56.

Kundera, Milan and David Rieff. "Esch is Luther." *Review of Contemporary Fiction* 8, no. 2 (1988): 266–72.

Kupferberg, Feiwel. "The Other Postmodernism." *Partisan Review.* 58, no. 3 (1991): 541–44.

Lemaitre, Monique J. "Territorialidad y transgresión en *Gringo viejo*, de Carlos Fuentes." *Revista Iberoamericana* 53 (1987): 954–63.

Levine, Susan F. "The Lesson of the Quijote in the Works of Carlos Fuentes and Juan Goytisolo." *Journal of Spanish Studies: Twentieth Century* 7 (1979): 173–85.

———. "The Pyramid and the Volcano: Carlos Fuentes' *Cambio de piel* and Malcolm Lowry's *Under the Volcano*." *Mester* 11 (1982): 25–40.

——— and Stuart Levine. "Poe and Fuentes: The Reader's Prerogatives." *Comparative Literature* 36 (1984): 34–53.

Loveluck, Juan, and Issac Levy, eds. *Simposio Carlos Fuentes: Actas.* University of South Carolina Press, Department of Foreign Languages and Literatures: Hispanic Studies, no. 2. Columbia: 1980.

Lyotard, Jean-Francois. *The Postmodern Condition.* Minneapolis: University of Minnesota Press, 1984.

Meacham, Cherie. "The Process of Dialogue in *Gringo viejo*." *Hispanic Journal* 10, no. 2 (1989): 127–37.

Mendelson, Edward. "*Gravity's Rainbow.*" *Mindful Pleasures.* Edited by George Levine and David Leverenz. Boston: Little, Brown, 1976.

Meyer-Minnemann, Klaus. "Narración homodiegética y 'segunda persona': *Cambio de piel* de Carlos Fuentes." *Acta Literaria* 9 (1984): 5–27.

McCaffey, Larry, ed. *Postmodern Fiction: A Bio-Bibliographic Guide.* New York, Greenwood: 1986.

McCracken, Ellen. "Metaplagiarism and the Critic's Role as Detective: Ricardo Piglia's Reinvention of Roberto Arlt." *PMLA* 106, no. 5 (1991): 1071–82.

McHale, Brian. *Postmodernist Fiction.* New York: Methuen, 1987.

Ortega, Julio. "*Christopher Unborn*: Rage and Laughter." *Review of Contemporary Fiction* 8, no. 2 (1988): 285–91.

Paley Francescato, Martha. "*Distant Relations*: Chronicle of Various Close Readings." *World Literature Today* 57 (1983): 590–94.

Parkinson Zamora, Lois. "Magic Realism and Fantastic History: Carlos Fuentes' *Terra Nostra* and Giambattista Vico's *The New Science*." *Review of Contemporary Fiction* 8, no. 2 (1988): 249–56.

———. "Novels and Newspapers in the Americas." *Novel* 23 (1989): 44–62.

Parsons, Robert A. "The Allegorical Dimension of Carlos Fuentes' *Terra Nostra.*" *Hispanic Journal* 7, no. 2 (1986): 93–99.

———. "The 'Vision of Horror' or 'Opposing Self': The Double in Three Novels by Carlos Fuentes." *Journal of Evolutionary Psychology* 8 (1987): 105–14.

Paz, Octavio. "The Question of Carlos Fuentes." *Review of Contemporary Fiction* 8, no. 2 (1988): 186–88.

Peden, Margaret Sayers. "Forking Paths, Infinite Novels, Ultimate Narrators." In *Carlos Fuentes: A Critical View*, edited by Robert Brody and Charles Rossman. Austin: University of Texas Press, 1982.

———. "A Reader's Guide to *Terra Nostra.*" *Latin American Literatures and Arts* 31 (1982): 42–48.

———. "*Terra Nostra*: Fact and Fiction." *The American Hispanist* 1, no. 1 (1975): 4–6.

Ramírez Mattei, Aida Elsa. "El nivel mítico-simbólico de lectura en la narrativa de Carlos Fuentes." *Revista de Estudios Hispánicos* 17–18 (1990–1991): 236–45.

Reed, Walter. *An Exemplary History of the Novel*. Chicago: University of Chicago Press, 1981.

Reeve, Richard. "Selected Bibliography (1949–1982)." *World Literature Today* 57, no. 4 (1983): 541–46.

Reyes-Tatinclaux, Leticia. "*Cristóbal Nonato*, ¿descubri-miento o clausura del Nuevo Mundo?." *Revista de Crítica Literaria Latinoamericana* 15, no. 30 (1989): 99–104.

Roy, Joaquín. "Historia, biografía, cine y ficción." *Revista de Crítica Literaria Latinoamericana* 2 semestre (1990): 147–64.

Salcedo, Fernando F. "Los 'monjes': Personajes claves en *Cambio de piel* de Carlos Fuentes." *Hispanófila*. 25, no. 75 (1982): 69–82.

Sarduy, Severo. "Baroque and Neobaroque." In *Latin America in its Literature*, edited by César Fernández Moreno and translated by Mary C. Berg. New York: Homes and Meier, 1980.

———. *Ensayos generales sobre el barroco*. Mexico: Fondo de Cultura Económica, 1987.

Schaffer, Susan. "The Development of the Double in Selected Works of Carlos Fuentes." *Mester* 6 (1977): 81–86.

Shaw, Donald L. "Narrative Arrangement in *La muerte deArtemio Cruz.*" In *Contemporary Latin American Fiction*, edited by Salvador Bacarisse. Edinburgh: Scottish Academic Press, 1980: 34–47.

———. *Nueva narrativa hispanoamericana*. Madrid: Cátedra, 1985.

———. "Which Was the First Novel of the Boom?" *Modern Language Review* 89, no. 2 (1994): 360–71.

Stark, John O. *The Literature of Exhaustion*. Durham: Duke University Press, 1974.

Stavans, Ilan. "The Latin American Connection." *Review of Contemporary Fiction* 10 (1990): 35–41.

Swanson, Philip, ed. *Landmarks in Modern Latin American Fiction*. London: Routledge, 1990.

Swietlicki, Catherine. "Doubling, Reincarnation, and Cosmic Order in *Terra Nostra*." *Hispanófila* 27, no. 1 (1983): 93–104.

———. "*Terra Nostra*: Carlos Fuentes' Kabbalistic World." *Symposium* 35, no. 2 (1981): 155–67.

Tani, Stefano. *The Doomed Detective: The Contribution of the Detective Novel to Postmodern American and Italian Fiction*. Carbondale: Southern Illinois University Press, 1984.

Tierney-Tello, Mary-Beth. "Re-Making the Margins: From Subalterity to Subjectivity in Diamela Eltit's *Por la patria*." *Monographic Review/Revista Monográfica* 8 (1992): 205–22.

Tittler, Jonathan. "*Cambio de piel/Zona sagrada*: Trans-figuration in Carlos Fuentes." *World Literature Today* 57, no. 4 (1983): 583–90.

———. "*Gringo viejo/The Old Gringo*." *Review of Contemporary Fiction* 8, no. 2 (1988): 241–48.

Toscano, Nicolás. "*Terra Nostra* y la pintura." *Cuadernos Americanos* 4 (1990): 192–98.

Ulloa, Leonor Alvarez de and Justo C. Ulloa. "La función del fragmento en *Colibrí* de Sarduy." *Modern Language Notes* 109 (1994): 268–82.

Van Delden, Maarten. "Carlos Fuentes: From Identity to Alternativity." *Modern Language Notes* 108, no. 2 (1993): 331–46.

———. "Carlos Fuentes' *Agua quemada*: The Nation as Unimaginable Community." *Latin American Literary Review* 21, no. 42 (1993): 57–69.

———. "The Banquets of Civilization: The Idea of Ancient Greece in Rodó, Reyes and Fuentes." *Annals of Scholarship* 7, no. 3 (1990): 303–21.

———. "Myth, Contingency, and Revolution in Carlos Fuentes' *La región más transparente*." *Comparative Literature* 43, no. 4 (1991): 326–45.

———. "Postmodernism and the Culture of the 1960's: The Examples of Carlos Fuentes and Thomas Pynchon." Ph.D. diss., Columbia University, 1991. Abstract in *Dissertation Abstracts International* 52 (1991): 532A.

———. "The View from the Womb." Review of *Cristóbal Nonato*, by Carlos Fuentes. *New Leader*, 27 November, 1989, 17–18.

Volek, Emil. "Realismo mágico entre la modernidad y la postmodernidad: hacia una remodelización cultural y discursiva de la nueva narrativa hispanoamericana." *Inti* 30 (1990): 3–20.

Williams, Raymond L. "After Foucault: On the Future of Indo-Afro-Iberoamerican Studies." *Latin American Literary Review* 20, no. 40 (1992): 120–24.

———. "Observaciones sobre el doble en *Terra Nostra*. In *Simposio Carlos Fuentes: Actas*, edited by Juan Loveluck and Issac Levy. University of South Carolina: Hispanic Studies, no. 2. Columbia, 1980: 175–83.

———. "The Reader and the Recent Novels of Gustavo Sainz." *Hispania* 65, no. 3 (1982): 383–87.

Williams, Shirley A. "The Quest for Quetzalcoatl and Total Fiction." *Hispanic Journal* 8, no. 1 (Fall 1986): 109–24.

Wilson, S. R. "Review of *La cabeza de la hidra*." *Journal of Spanish Studies: Twentieth Century* 7 (1979): 107–10.

Index

149

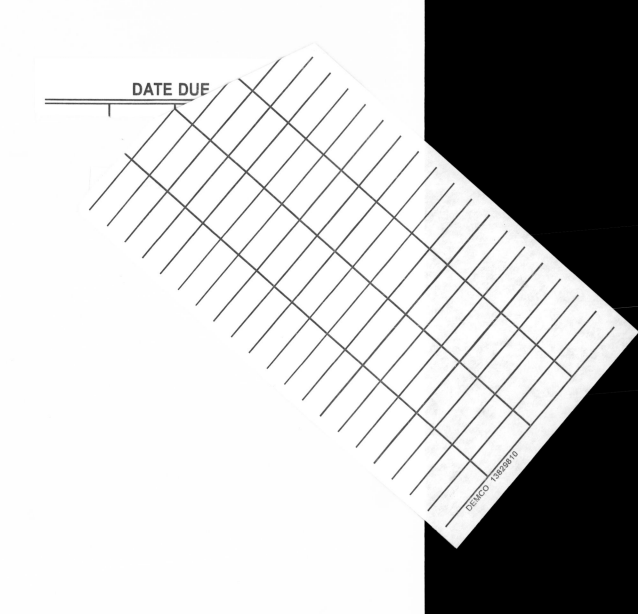

DATE DUE